*Building Youth Is Better
Than Mending Men!*

Building Youth Is Better Than Mending Men!

by
Dr. Ron Reilly

Sword of the Lord Publishers
MURFREESBORO, TENNESSEE 37130

Printed in The United States of America

Acknowledgements

Many people over the years have been a tremendous help to this author. The few mentioned below were my fellow-helpers as I endeavored to pen *Building Youth Is Better Than Mending Men*.

Mr. Charles Schaefer and Mrs. Doris Erickson were invaluable to me as they proofread, corrected and incorporated my thoughts in a manner which would be correct and proper. Mrs. Nancy Reilly is acknowledged for her chapter, "The Youth Director's Wife—Help or Hindrance?" And I am grateful to Mr. Gary Caudle for his thoughts and insights on the chapter, "Banquets."

My book is an accumulation of knowledge gained in my years as Youth Director in the same local church. I truly believe if what one reads in this book is applied to the lives of young people today through youth ministries, we will be able to build our youth to be able and spiritual men for tomorrow.

Dr. Ron Reilly
Founder-President
AMBASSADORS FOR CHRIST
NATIONAL MINISTRIES, INC.

Dedication

To Nancy, who during her teenage years gave me my first gospel witness and because of her consistent testimony and prayers led me to a saving knowledge of Jesus Christ.

Later as my wife, she has been my constant companion, my helpmeet, my encouragement. For over thirteen years she labored with me in the same church and helps me even today to carry my burden of reaching the youth of America.

Table of Contents

Introduction

The perils and problems of being a teenager take on an entirely different perspective when considered in light of Paul's admonition, "Let no man despise thy youth. . .be thou an example of the believer. . . ." How encouraging is this mandate to a Christian young person who aspires to please the Lord!

But knowing *how* to be an example is not always easy during the difficult adolescent years. In today's complex world, young people are looking for answers to the problems they face daily in trying to live for the Lord. Every pastor, youth director, and Sunday school teacher of teenagers has a solemn and sacred responsibility before the Lord to take advantage of the tools that God has provided for the fulfillment of His task.

One of these tools is the book entitled *Building Youth Is Better Than Mending Men.* The author, Dr. Ron Reilly, is one of the outstanding youth leaders in the nation and an expert in coping with problems peculiar to teenagers. For more than thirteen years he served on our staff at Trinity Baptist Church as the Youth Director, and was also on the faculty of Trinity Baptist College for five years. He is, in my opinion, uniquely qualified to write such a book which draws extensively from his rich and vast experience.

The primary value of this book is its usefulness as a manual for youth ministry in the local church. Beginning with the all-important aspect of a scriptural philosophy, the author transfers his ideas and concepts from the abstract to the concrete in such a pragmatic way that even a novice in youth work can be helped. The discerning reader will recognize that the insights, methodology and success statistics shared by Dr. Reilly are not offered with the probability of hoping that they will work but rather are humbly submitted as proof of a ministry that *has* worked!

Few men in the highly specialized field of youth ministry have enjoyed the God-given wisdom, the extensive and varied experience, and the respect and esteem of pastors and youth directors as has Dr. Reilly. He is an authority in his field, a trusted counselor of young people, the preacher's friend. I predict a wide use and great circulation of this book.

Dr. Bob Gray
Pastor, Trinity Baptist Church
Founder-President, Trinity
Baptist College

Preface

My philosophy of a successful youth ministry as expressed in this book, *Building Youth Is Better than Mending Men,* is as follows: True success in youth work is not measured by the facilities erected for the teenagers, but by the lives of young people who live for God as teenagers and later as adults.

The lie that Christian teens will probably dabble in the "world" originates in Hell. It is heartbreaking to see adults, who as saved teenagers "sowed their wild oats," now desperately striving to be the people God intended them to be. In nearly all of such cases with which I have been acquainted, the adults never reach their full potential for the Lord.

The illustration gives a complete analysis of the youth ministry in the local church and shows how it functions within the total church and youth ministry.

Notice, the pastor is the leader of the church ministry. The outside circle of the wheel illustrates the total ministry of the local church program of which the young people are members under the ultimate authority of the pastor.

The second circle pictures the total youth ministry in the local church. In this total ministry, the youth director ministers to all of his young people.

The third circle of the wheel reveals the actual function of the youth group itself. Notice, in the "youth ministry" the youth director ministers to as many teenagers as he can; but in the "youth group," he "works" closely with "a very few." This is not to suggest that the youth director is selective with whom he "works," but rather that the young people themselves elect to allow their leader to work with them.

The inner circle (No. 1) describes the purposes for which the youth group is functioning.

By applying the principle listed in the Youth Ministry Success Wheel, a youth leader can see his young people be used of God during and after their teen years.

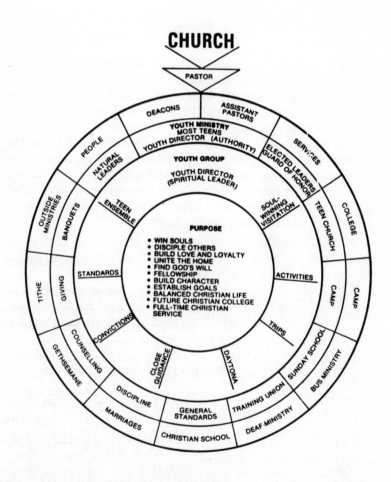

1 — The Birth

Before getting into the practical part of this book, I believe it is vital to relate the sequence of events which occurred in my life that led me into a ministry of working with teenagers.

Throughout my childhood and teen years, I was reared as a devout Roman Catholic. Even though I was taught to be religious, I had never heard the Gospel. I was an altar boy in the Catholic church, and my family never missed Mass unless for illness.

When I graduated from high school, I received a football scholarship to attend Eastern Montana College in Billings, Montana.

During the Christmas holidays of that first year of college, I met a Christian teenage girl who witnessed to me about the Lord. Through much prayer and dedication to Christ, she led me to the Lord.

After I was saved, my whole life changed. Nancy—the young lady who led me to the Lord—and I started attending a church in my hometown. The pastor was Dr. Wally Beebe. Under Dr. Beebe's ministry, I grew spiritually and learned how to win souls. Nancy was a great help. After Nancy and I married, Dr. Beebe influenced me to attend Bob Jones University.

After graduating, I was again influenced by Dr. Beebe who was at that time an assistant pastor of Trinity Baptist Church in Jacksonville, Florida, where Dr. Bob Gray is now the pastor. Dr. Beebe asked me and my wife to visit the church and invited us to work in the church camp for two weeks during the summer.

While at camp, I became acquainted with some young people. The Lord used one sixteen-year-old boy to burden my heart for the teenagers of Trinity Baptist Church in Jacksonville, Florida. At that time the church could not financially support any additional staff members, but desperately needed someone to work with teenagers. Not feeling that I was the one to fill the position, my wife and I returned to our home.

The night we were to leave Jacksonville, Phil Brown, the sixteen-year-old boy, met me in the back of the church. After shaking my hand, he started to cry and said, "Please come back, Brother Reilly; we need you here." I never forgot those words, and three months later the Lord used what he said to burden my heart to work with teenagers at Trinity Baptist Church.

After moving to Jacksonville, I got a job during the week and worked with teenagers on weekends. After one year, the church employed me full time. That was over thirteen years ago, and the Lord has blessed our ministry.

I believe that God can and will use teenagers and will honor them in His will for the future.

My wife, Nancy, faithfully stands by my side as my best helper.

Phil Brown graduated from Bob Jones University with a Master's Degree and is now Dean of Students at Trinity Baptist College. To God be the glory!

Throughout this book soul winning is stressed. It is the backbone upon which a youth ministry must be built if it is to successfully help teenagers in their Christian lives. The main theme of this book is not the building of a great youth program, but the building of great lives.

2 — Youth Visitation Program

In the years that I have served as youth director at Trinity Baptist Church, I have been asked repeatedly two questions: "Can teenagers really win souls?" and, "How do you get teenagers involved in winning souls?"

First, let me state that after working with teenagers and seeing them win thousands to Christ over these several years, I am convinced that teenagers *can win souls* and that they *can become totally involved* in witnessing for the Lord Jesus Christ.

In this chapter let me share those principles which will enable youth directors to involve their young people in a successful youth visitation program.

It is of utmost importance that a youth director understand the purposes for involving youth in a visitation ministry. The director himself must be totally convinced if he is to impart to his young people the need for visitation. In Matthew 28:19,20, Jesus commanded:

"Go ye therefore, and teach all nations, baptizing them in the name of the Father, and of the Son, and of the Holy Ghost: Teaching them to observe all things whatsoever I have commanded you: and, lo, I am with you alway, even unto the end of the world. Amen."

Again in Mark 16:15:

"And he said unto them, Go ye into all the world, and preach the gospel to every creature."

Teenagers are commanded to win souls and be faithful witnesses. The visitation program provides for every teenager the opportunity to obey the command of God.

Second, the visitation program provides the training necessary for teenagers to be able to utilize effectively the Bible plan of soul winning. Jesus taught that witnessing is to be from "house to house," "two by two," and is to reach into the "highways and hedges." It is important that young people be instructed in the plan of God.

Third, the youth visitation program allows young people to learn how to win souls by observing others who witness.

Last, the purpose of the program is to help the teenager grow spiritually by enabling him, with the help of the youth ministry, to obey God's command. It is vitally important that young people learn to obey God now in order that they might trust His guidance in the future as they train for His service.

In order to be successful soul winners, young people must have some convictions. Second Timothy 2:19-22 states:

"Nevertheless the foundation of God standeth sure, having this seal, The Lord knoweth them that are his. And, Let every one that nameth the name of Christ depart from iniquity. But in a great house there are not only vessels of gold and of silver, but also of wood and of earth; and some to honour, and some to dishonour. If a man therefore purge himself from these, he shall be a vessel unto honour, sanctified, and meet for the master's use, and prepared unto every good work. Flee also youthful lusts: but follow righteousness, faith, charity, peace, with them that call on the Lord out of a pure heart."

A teenager must be a clean vessel and his life must be empty of sin—impure thoughts, wrong actions, bad attitudes, selfish desires. A young person who has sin in his heart will not know the success that comes from a heart cleansed by God. A soul winner must also have a heart burdened for souls. Psalm 126:6 says: "He that goeth forth and weepeth, bearing precious seed, shall doubtless come again with rejoicing, bringing his sheaves with him." How vital it is that teens be emptied, cleansed and Spirit-filled.

To be successful, every visitation program must have a plan. The group must have a definite, designated time for going soul winning and a specific area to visit. Young people who are not yet prepared to do the talking should be assigned with someone who is. Boys should be assigned with boys, girls with girls, and each to a specific team to avoid confusion. Adult chaperones should accompany the teams to insure the safety of each one. Young people should meet together before embarking on visitation, a song sung, testimonies of past blessings shared, and prayers offered to prepare their hearts.

It is especially important that a youth visitation program have and insist upon standards. Young people should look their best before leaving the church—clean clothing and a neat appearance. Girls' dresses should be the proper length, boys' hair cut to meet Christian standards. Personal hygiene is important, and each should do everything necessary to make a good impression for the Lord. After good standards have been established, be careful to maintain them, and do not change them!

The conduct of young people who are involved in witnessing should be above reproach. They should be kind, courteous and show a sincere concern for the lost. They should be personable and display good sense and good judgment in handling difficult situations. A young person needs to be taught these basic concepts, and the visitation program offers the opportunity of instructing tomorrow's leaders.

The equipment needed for a youth visitation program is not expensive, and it can be easily obtained. A director needs a New Testament, a collection of teen visitation cards, gospel tracts, pens or pencils, a card file containing the name of every teenager in the youth group, and a master bus list. Each young person is given several visitation cards to use in visiting. A master bus list contains the name of every teenager involved in the visitation and gives the number of the team to which he is assigned. It also states which bus he is riding and with whom he is visiting. These simple aids provide assistance and will help the visitation to be conducted orderly.

In order to help young people witness more effectively from door to door, they need to be taught certain guidelines. Only *one* person should do the talking. The speaker always introduces himself and the name of his partner at the doorway, along with the name of his church. Being polite, he proceeds to the main reason for their visit by asking, "If you died tonight, would you go to Heaven?" The response will determine the future course of the conversation.

Find some way to get the individual to realize his lost condition. He may try to change the subject, but the soul winner must remain steadfast in his approach. He must be conscious of his need for the filling of the Holy Spirit as stated in Ephesians 5:18: "And be not drunk with wine, wherein is excess; but be filled with the Spirit."

After showing the individual from the Word of God that he is a sinner (Rom. 3:10; 3:23), the teenager needs to show the price of sin as is revealed in Romans 5:12 and 6:23. It is extremely important now to show the lost one that the price has been paid for his sin (Rom. 5:8). Romans 6:23b, John 1:12, Romans 10:13, and Revelation 3:20 may be used to show the person how to receive Christ as his Saviour.

After a person accepts Jesus, he should be left with words of assurance such as are found in I John 5:12,13 and Hebrews 13:5b.

The results of a youth visitation program are numerous. How thrilling to see young people become active soul winners! Many of their own disciplinary problems will be solved. Young people will become "soul-conscious" and will be drawn closer to the Lord as they see those they have won walk down the aisle of the church to make a public profession.

Soul winning helps teenagers find the right kind of fellowship. They begin to develop a unity in the youth group and come to have a greater concern for each other.

Soul winning builds character and gives teens a boldness they never had before.

Soul winning will help young people have a better relationship with their parents and other family members. In short, it will bring the blessing of God upon the teenager's life.

Youth director, it is important that you begin a visitation program as soon as possible. It is not necessary to have a large number of young people. Begin with *one* if that is all you have.

Teach the principles of soul winning, develop a definite program, set up Christian standards, and be faithful to train new ones year after year. "And let us not be weary in well doing: for in due season we shall reap, if we faint not" (Gal. 6:9). When we first started the teen visitation program at Trinity we had eight or ten come to learn how to win souls and participate in the visitation program.

Yes, I am convinced that teenagers can win souls. It was a teenage girl who first witnessed to me and led me to a saving knowledge of Jesus Christ. I married that girl and now weekly both of us are privileged to see many teenagers experience the blessing of winning souls.

RULES FOR TEEN VISITATION

1. The radio is NOT to be on going or coming back from visitation.

2. DON'T allow any gossip.

3. KNOW where the teenagers are at ALL times.

4. Do NOT stop ANY PLACE to eat, drink or go to a restroom. Our purpose is to win souls.

5. Be a FRIEND to teenagers, but don't go down to their level.

6. NO foolishness will be tolerated. Firm discipline is to be practiced at ALL times.

7. NO physical contact between boys and girls.

8. Start back to the church no later than 9:00 p.m. but not before 8:45 p.m.

9. DON'T let the teenagers out any place but at the church.

10. When you return to the church, check in and give the team results.

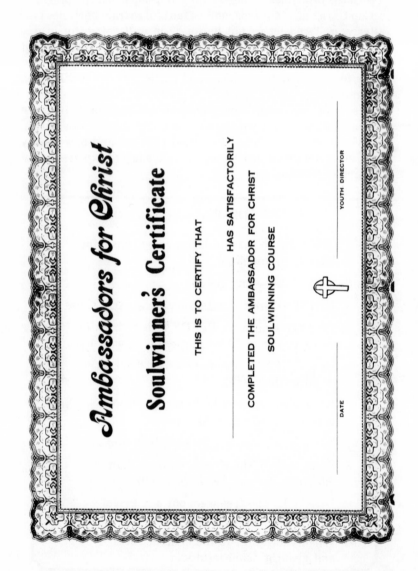

Ambassadors for Christ

Soulwinners' Certificate

THIS IS TO CERTIFY THAT

_____ HAS SATISFACTORILY

COMPLETED THE AMBASSADOR FOR CHRIST

SOULWINNING COURSE

_____
DATE

_____
YOUTH DIRECTOR

SOUL WINNERS CLUB

Date_____

Name_____

  I. SOULS SAVED (Sept. 1, 1977 - Dec. 4, 1977) _____

 II. HOW MANY PEOPLE HAVE YOU WITNESSED TO THIS
     PAST WEEK?_____

III. BIBLE READING (For the past week)

     Mon._____ Tues._____ Wed._____ Thurs._____
     Fri._____ Sat._____ Sun._____

 IV. YOUTH ACTIVITIES MISSED (Sept. 1, 1977 - Dec. 4, 1977)

     _____

  V. TEENAGE VISITATION--HAVE YOU MISSED ANY THE PAST
     MONTH?

     How many?_____ Excuse_____

AMBASSADORS FOR CHRIST

SOUL WINNERS CLUB

DIRECTOR, DR. RON REILLY

QUALIFICATIONS:
  I.   Faithful to all things.
 II.   Read Bible daily.
III.   Witness to at least six people a week.
 IV.   Everyone starts by winning souls.
  V.   Must attend all club meetings.

1 BRONZE STAR	25 souls
2 BRONZE STARS	50 souls
3 BRONZE STARS	75 souls
1 SILVER STAR	100 souls
2 SILVER STARS	150 souls
3 SILVER STARS	200 souls
4 SILVER STARS	250 souls
GOLD STAR	300 souls
GOLD STAR WITH HONORS	350 souls
GOLD STAR WITH HIGHEST HONORS	400 souls and up
DISTINGUISHED MEDAL OF HONOR	Having a convert make a profession of faith
SOUL WINNER'S CROWN	Soul saved, joined church & involved in youth group (discipling a teen)

A trip to Atlanta will be awarded to any Senior High young person who reaches the Gold Star level, and to all seventh and eighth graders who reach the three Silver Star level.

A.   Any seventh or eighth grader who reaches the three Silver Star level may go to the annual Teen Banquet free; any Senior High who reaches the Gold Star level may go to the annual Teen Banquet free.

B.   A free trip to Atlanta will be awarded the Senior High young person who reaches the Gold Star with Highest Honors level.

C.   Any young person who receives two Distinguished Medals of Honor may go on the Atlanta trip.

D.   Any young person who receives a Soul Winners Crown and one Silver Star will qualify to go on the trip, and his motel charges will be paid.

I ACCEPT THE ABOVE QUALIFICATIONS, AND DESIRE TO BECOME A MEMBER OF THE SOUL WINNERS CLUB. AT ANY TIME I FAIL TO MEET THE ABOVE QUALIFICATIONS, I EXPECT TO BE REMOVED FROM THE CLUB.

_____

CLUB MEMBER'S SIGNATURE

A.F.C.   MEMBERSHIP CARD

Teenage Soulwinners Club

Member

**AN OUTREACH OF THE AMBASSADOR
FOR CHRIST YOUTH MINISTRY**

Youth Director

800 Hammond Blvd., Jacksonville, Fla.   Phone 786-5320
Good thru Aug., 1978

This certifies that _____
is a:

1 Bronze Star Soulwinner	25 souls
2 Bronze Stars Soulwinner	50 souls
3 Bronze Stars Soulwinner	75 souls
1 Silver Star Soulwinner	100 souls
2 Silver Stars Soulwinner	150 souls
3 Silver Stars Soulwinner	200 souls
4 Silver Stars Soulwinner	250 souls
Gold Star Soulwinner	300 souls
Gold Star With Honors	350 souls
Gold Star Highest Honors	400 souls

*This club has high Christian standards with a bur-
den to reach lost teenagers with the Gospel of Jesus
Christ.*

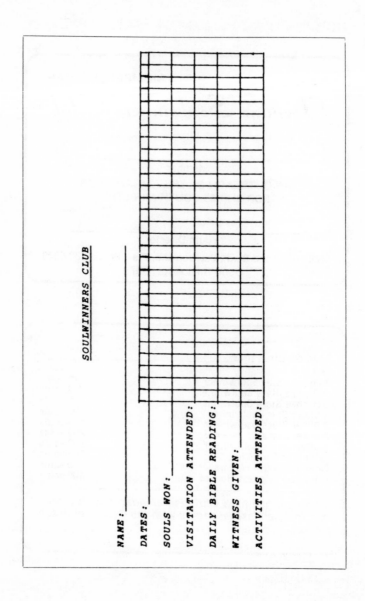

SOULWINNERS CLUB

NAME: _____

DATES: _____

SOULS WON: _____

VISITATION ATTENDED:

DAILY BIBLE READING:

WITNESS GIVEN:

ACTIVITIES ATTENDED:

HOW TO START A TEENAGE SOUL-WINNING VISITATION PROGRAM

Introduction:

The purpose of a Youth Visitation Program is to give Christian teenagers in the church the opportunity to obey God's command, train them in the Bible plan for soul winning, and help them grow spiritually by obeying God's command.

I. TRAIN YOUNG PEOPLE TO WIN SOULS.

A. How to be a proper sacrifice:
   1. Be consecrated (have a clean vessel).
   2. Be separated (have strong standards).
B. How to present the proper service:
   1. Be familiar with the plan of salvation.
   2. Be filled with the Spirit.

II. ORGANIZE THE PROGRAM.

A. Set up a weekly visitation program.
   1. Have a special time and place to meet.
   2. Have testimonies and give instructions before going out.
   3. Have teams of four with an adult block chaperone for each team—two boys and two girls, if possible.
B. Set biblical standards and stick to them.
   1. Have standards on dress and appearance.
      Boys: short hair, ties.
      Girls: modest dresses (no higher than the knee).
   2. Maintain good conduct.
      Have good manners; be courteous and sincere.

III. TAKE YOUNG PEOPLE OUT SOUL WINNING.

A. For ten to fifteen teens, use a van; when over twenty, use a bus. The teenagers should be seated on the bus in the order of the team, girls on one side, boys on the other.
B. Have a designated area for each team.
   1. Shopping centers.

    2. House to house.

C. Have them go two by two, i.e., for house to house visitation, have two girls on one side of the street and two boys on the other.

D. Have the proper materials: New Testaments, teen visitation cards, gospel tracts, pen or pencil.

E. Have a basic plan for the young people to use:
    1. Introduce themselves.
    2. Ask, "If you were to die tonight, would you go to Heaven?"
    3. Go right into the plan of salvation.
    4. Get names and addresses of converts and follow them up.

IV. SET UP A SOUL WINNERS CLUB FOR YOUNG PEOPLE.

A. A Soul Winners Club can be used to:
    1. Help motivate teenagers to win souls.
    2. Recognize and reward their soul winning efforts.
    3. Emphasize the importance of soul winning in the youth group.
    4. Unify the group as to its goals and attitudes.

B. A Soul Winners Club should be based on certain qualifications and an award system. Special trips may be planned for the soul winners who really excel and earn the highest honors. (Example attached is an Ambassadors for Christ Soul Winners Club application sheet.)

Conclusion:

The results of a Youth Visitation Program are many: (1) teenagers become active soul winners; (2) many disciplinary problems are solved as teens grow in the Lord; (3) names of converts can be followed up by the soul winner, youth pastor, or bus captains; (4) people (especially young people) walk the aisle of the church service to make public profession of faith; and (5) teenagers become "soul conscious."

DISCIPLED PERSON

DISCIPLER

				DATE
				FIRST CONTACT
				SALVATION
				BAPTIZED
				PUBLIC PROFESSION
				SUNDAY MORNING
				SUNDAY EVENING
				WEDNESDAY EVENING
				NO. OF CONTACTS
				ACTIVITY ATTENDANCE
				VISITATION
				DEVOTIONS
				PRAYER REQUESTS

3 — Weekly Youth Activities—
"Activities or Parties?"

The most important phase of all our youth program is the weekly activity provided for both Junior and Senior High teenagers. I say that because it involves a concentrated effort to build a balanced Christian teenager.

When many churches provide some kind of parties for their youth, they feel they have really done something for them. But churches are "off the track" when they hold to this kind of concept. They have simply provided something to keep the teen out of trouble or to clear his conscience. This philosophy will never get the job done, will not accomplish the end results of building a life. It will only provide something temporary and appealing to the flesh but do nothing spiritually for the teen.

In our youth ministry we never have what we refer to as "parties." We always conduct "youth activities" strictly for the teenager, each designed to meet the goal of developing a balanced life. To reach the whole teenager, we must deal with three distinct aspects of his life: the physical, the emotional, the spiritual.

The **physical** aspect can be easily met by providing wholesome, energetic activities. Going bowling, riding horses, having a progressive supper or going on a scavenger hunt are generally successful ones.

The **emotional** aspect is developed by his participating in good, clean fellowship and by having a good time with other teens in a well-planned event.

The **spiritual** aspect is accomplished by promoting soul winning on every activity and by the youth director bringing a challenging message from the Word of God.

Many youth programs do much with the physical, touch on the emotional, but fail to develop the spiritual part. Teenagers in fundamental churches are usually instructed to win souls, but many times the youth leader fails to teach how to win souls or to get them involved in witnessing. Therefore, the main thrust of every activity should be soul winning.

For example, during a "progressive supper" activity, we involve them in soul winning. The teens are divided into teams, and each team is accompanied by an adult driver. The young people witness to at least ten people before going to the first house for appetizers. Before arriving at the second house for salad, they witness to ten more individuals. Ten more are dealt with before the main course, and finally ten more hear the Gospel before dessert. On the occasion of one progressive breakfast, our Senior High young people led 218 people to Christ.

Soul winning is a MUST for every youth activity if the spiritual life is to be enhanced.

Youth leader, when you begin a program of youth activities, the following steps should be taken:

1. Set up a calendar of events at least three months in advance.
2. Have the calendar approved by the pastor.
3. Coordinate the calendar with the church schedule to avoid conflicts.
4. Give a copy of the schedule to each teenager.
5. Advertise the activity in the church bulletin.
6. Announce the activity in the teen Sunday school classes, in the teen training union, and in the church services.
7. Teach the young people to be faithful to the activities by teaching and preaching the Bible.
8. Be consistent; do not delete a scheduled activity.

Activities should be planned out carefully, and everything needed obtained in advance. It is important that proper help be obtained before the activity to make it a success. The youth leader must be on time, must start on time, must end on time in order to gain the confidence of parents.

During the activity, it is the leader's responsibility to be always on top of everything. Know where the young people are and what they are doing. Every visitor should receive a personal welcome, and every teen should be greeted by the leader at some time during the activity.

Don't allow boys and girls to date, since this is not a dating time. Instead, separate close friends in order to help promote a unity within the group and to encourage new friendships. Don't overly expose them to worldly influences but encourage them to take a separated stand.

The youth leader must be familiar with every activity and endeavor to make them exciting for all in his group.

All activities can and should be a blessing in a teenager's life. They can help develop him physically, emotionally, and spiritually, as well as bring him rewards at the judgment seat of Christ.

HOW TO HAVE SOUL-WINNING YOUTH ACTIVITIES

Introduction:

Soul winning is the key for building the right kind of youth group. It will produce in them an amazing growth, as well as growth in the kingdom of God through the precious souls they win to Christ.

I. THE PRIORITY OF SOUL WINNING.

Soul winning should be considered as typical of your weekly activities.

A. Make soul winning a part of every activity.

B. Have few exceptions to this rule, i.e., Halloween costume activities, youth rallies, etc.

C. Some activities may consist solely of a soul-winning thrust, with a picnic afterward.

II. THE PLACE FOR SOUL WINNING.

A. Go where the lost are:
   1. Shopping centers.
   2. Carnivals.
   3. Street corners.
   4. Beach Boardwalk.
   5. Downtown.
   6. Parks.
B. Go with a purpose in mind:
   1. To reach the lost with the plan of salvation.
   2. To get them to trust Christ on the spot.
   3. To get the names and addresses of converts and follow them up.
C. Set a goal for each team:
   1. Teams should consist of two boys and two girls.
   2. Each team should have a goal of a certain number of converts.

III. THE PROSPERITY OF THE SOUL-WINNING YOUTH GROUP.

A. Soul winning will purify the members of your youth group.
   1. It will cause them to get sin out of their lives.
   2. It will create in them a spiritual hunger for training in the Word of God.
B. Soul winning will unify the members of your youth group.
   1. It will bring them closer together and create a "team spirit."
   2. It will help them to want to meet each other's needs.
C. Soul winning will give the other aspects of the activity more meaning.
   1. The teenagers will appreciate the physical recreation as a time of letting off tension.

   2. Young people will be able to handle the social aspect of their lives better after seeing the importance of a close walk with God in soul winning.

IV. SOME PROSPECTS FOR SOUL-WINNING ACTIVITIES.
   A. Planning a soul-winning activity:
      1. If at all possible, take the teens out on a bus.
      2. Get them excited about reaching their soul-winning goals.
      3. Put talkers with non-talkers and balance the teams as much as possible.
      4. Plan for a time of physical and social fun afterward.
      5. Set the right standards.
         (Activities should involve mainly your own teens; visitors should be expected to abide by your own standards. Other activities which are not for the purpose of soul winning, such as youth rallies, etc., may be used to reach more visitors.)
         a. Never allow physical contact between boys and girls.
         b. Boys should not have long hair.
         c. Girls should wear dresses no higher than the knee. For some rough activities girls may be allowed to wear culottes.
   B. Ideas for soul-winning activities:
      1. Progressive Supper (witness before each house; for this activity put teams in cars driven by adults).
      2. Scavenger Hunt.
      3. Bowling (go witnessing first).
      4. Putt-Putt (go witnessing first).

Conclusion:
   A balanced Christian life must begin with the proper emphasis on soul winning. Teenagers need and want challenges, and they should be able to find them within the framework of the youth ministry of the local church.

4 — Bible Clubs in Public Schools and on Bus Routes

Bible clubs are a vital part of a youth ministry. The purpose of these clubs is not only to reach the lost but also to provide an additional opportunity for their spiritual growth. In the past years, we have established two different types of Bible clubs—the clubs which reach into the public schools and those composed of teens from various bus routes of the church.

One way of reaching into the public schools has been by means of Bible clubs. The most effective way to begin a Bible club is to use a nucleus of young people from one's church who attend the public school.

Our Bible club ministry began in Jacksonville with one of our Junior High boys, Scotty Hollenbeck, who had a burden to reach the young people in his school. He talked with me about it, and the Lord led us to begin the club in a home near the school. Since this was not an ideal location, I asked the principal if it might be possible to use a room in the school, assuring him that I was not representing any particular denomination but only trying to help young people. He granted permission for the room, and we made plans to begin the club, meeting every Monday morning before school. Because of the Lord's blessing, I started three other clubs in public high schools on that same day. At a later time, three more clubs were begun, and we saw many young people saved.

In our Bible club at Lee High, the son of the mayor of Jacksonville accepted the Lord as his Saviour. Because of our contact with him, I had the privilege of leading his mother to the Lord in her home.

At Forrest High, teenagers were faithful to invite visitors. One day Kevin was brought to the club by his best friend. This crippled boy, a Roman Catholic, came in a wheelchair. He raised his hand indicating a desire to be saved, but he would not make a decision.

After the fifth week, Scotty Hollenbeck took Kevin to another room after the service and led him to the Lord. Later when Scott asked Kevin why he had waited so long to accept the Lord, Kevin explained that he had heard the young people in the club were "different" from unsaved teens, and he was watching to determine if they really were different. When he accepted Christ, he found that Christ was able to change lives—especially his own! Kevin was faithful and grew spiritually.

Near the end of the school year, as Kevin's best friend was pushing him down the hall of the school, the wheelchair went out of control at a corner and went down a steep ramp. Kevin's body flew out of his chair and hit the ground. Four hours later, Kevin died in a local hospital.

What a shock his death was to all who knew him! How we praised the Lord that Kevin was now in Heaven! How thankful I am for those young people who were "different" and let their light shine (Matt. 5:14). I do not believe Kevin would have been saved had those young people not lived for Jesus Christ.

These are just some of the results that we have seen because of Bible clubs. Many were reached with the Gospel, and many have continued to serve the Lord. Phil Huffman was reached through the Forrest High School Bible Club. He later graduated from Tennessee Temple University and now teaches in Trinity Christian Academy.

Bible clubs are one of the most effective ways of reaching young people. I would like to challenge every youth director to start one in the public schools if at all possible.

In starting and maintaining a Bible club in the public schools, the following suggestions should prove helpful:

1. Visit the principal and secure permission to conduct the club.

2. Survey the school; be certain there are some Christian young people attending.
3. Begin and end the meetings on time in order to establish a good testimony.
4. Challenge the Christian young people to invite others to the club.
5. Keep the meetings evangelistic and deal with subjects which will interest and help teens.

Teenagers can be reached through other areas as well. Special assembly programs in the school reach great numbers in a limited amount of time. Bus routes provide many names of unsaved young people in the public schools. Bus captains, youth pastors, Christian teenagers make contacts with these teens as they visit their routes.

Another way of reaching the lost in our public schools is through the means of citywide youth banquets. By obtaining a nice meeting place, by inviting a "top-notch" speaker, and by advertising in the public schools and local stores, it is possible to reach many who are lost.

BIBLE CLUBS ON BUS ROUTES

I. HOW TO START A BIBLE CLUB.

A. Start with one club.
1. Direct it yourself.
2. Get it started right.
3. Keep it going right.
4. Make it accomplish your goals.
B. Start it on a particular bus route.
1. With teens that come on one of your bus routes.
2. Need to have backing of bus captain.
C. Have a place to meet.
1. Try to get a place on or near the bus route.

   2. Homes of people in your church who really want to
      help young people.
   3. A conference room in an apartment building.
   4. A garage.
   5. A family room in a house.
   6. A room large enough to hold them.
   7. A place free from disruptions.

II. PURPOSE OF BIBLE CLUB.

   A. To have another point of spiritual contact.
   B. To give them more spiritual growth on a personal level.
   C. To give them a burden to reach the lost.
   D. A place where they can bring friends to be saved.
   E. To provide an activity time for your bus teens.
   F. To give them something they can be a part of and call
      their own.

III. HOW TO OPERATE THE CLUB.

   A. The director is in control.
   B. Meet on a particular night—Example: Monday or Tues-
      day.
   C. Have a specific time to start and end—Example: 7:00
      p.m. to 8:30 p.m.
   D. Provide a ride for the teenagers.
   E. Get people to help pick them up. (Church people are
      provided with another area of service to the Lord.)
   F. Begin the service with good singing for teens.
   G. Have a good message.
      1. Director speaks.
      2. Have guest speakers.
      3. Don't speak too long.
   H. An invitation for lost and saved.
    I. Provide refreshments and time of fellowship (about fif-
      teen minutes) at the end.

IV. SOME THINGS TO TEACH IN CLUB.

   A. Christian convictions and standards.
   B. Soul winning.

C. Discipleship.

V. HAVE BY-LAWS FOR CLUB.

Example: The following is a list of the Ambassadors for Christ Bible Club By-Laws.

AMBASSADORS FOR CHRIST BIBLE CLUB BY-LAWS

I. All Bible clubs are a direct ministry of the Ambassadors for Christ Youth Ministry of Trinity Baptist Church, Jacksonville, Florida.

II. Purpose of each club is to provide an extra outreach to teenagers who come on our buses that they might receive additional spiritual help and grow in their Christian lives, and to reach the lost teenagers throughout the city.

III. Each Bible club will have its own director who in turn will be under the direction and leadership of Dr. Ron Reilly, Founder and Director of the Ambassadors for Christ Youth Ministry, and Mr. Clint Andrews, Bible Club Coordinator.

IV. All Bible clubs will teach subjects vital to the growth of the teen's spiritual life.

V. Once every quarter all Bible clubs will come together for a youth activity under the direction of Dr. Ron Reilly and with the assistance of all the Bible club directors.

VI. Standards of dress and conduct will be maintained and practiced by all Bible club members on any special trips or soul winning activities, such as:
A. Girls must wear dresses at all times no higher than the knee.
B. Boys must wear a clean, neat pair of pants with shirt and tie. Their hair must be cut neat and manly.
C. No physical contact between boys and girls tolerated.

VII. At the end of each year a plaque will be presented to one of the Bible clubs that will bear the title:

"MOST OUTSTANDING BIBLE CLUB OF THE YEAR"

VIII. There will be certain designated times for special Bible club meetings and all directors are to be present.
A. Plans will be made at this time.
B. Problems will be discussed.
C. Curriculum will be looked over and questions may be asked pertaining to its use.

IX. All Bible clubs will be invited to the special teen events such as Winter Youth Conference, banquet, Summer Camp, etc. We need to encourage young people to become more involved in these and all other activities sponsored by the Ambassadors for Christ Youth Ministry.

X. Bible club directors will be responsible for maintaining order, having moral and biblical standards in the club at all times. Any failure on the part of the Bible club director to fulfill his responsibility will result in his dismissal.

5 — Correlating the Church Activities With the Christian School

What a privilege it is for our teenagers to attend a Christian school where they receive instruction from the Word of God five days every week! This can and should be a real blessing in each teen's life. Because of the involvement of our teens in both church and school, it is necessary to follow certain guidelines.

First, the church and school must work together and strive for the same goals. Therefore, each must be willing to adjust for the benefit of the other.

The church should formulate its schedule of activities one year in advance. This schedule should be published and presented to the school administration. Likewise, the school must determine its schedule and publish a calendar of events coordinated with the church calendar. Each must make certain that there are no conflicts—either in the times of activities or in the costs of identical scheduled events.

Many times a real hardship is created at home because of so many church/school activities. Families need time together. In this day of inflation, both school and church must work at keeping costs down. So it is vitally important that church leaders and school administrators keep a clear line of communication in order to produce an efficient and successful operation.

The youth pastor plays a very important role in the ministry of the Christian school. It is his responsibility to challenge the young people to have a strong testimony for the Lord even in the Christian school. He must be willing to give spiritual help to any students in order to help meet their spiritual needs.

These goals can be accomplished by the youth pastor in

various ways. He should attend and preach in the chapel program. His title should be **Chaplain.** He could organize a Bible club for all students who wish to attend, conducted thirty minutes before school or at some other designated time.

The youth leader himself must be free to assist the students by providing them individual counseling. It is vital that he, in conducting personal counseling, do so with the permission of the school, and only by appointment.

By working together, both church and school can reap rewards of seeing young people's lives count for the Lord. However, it must be noted that many Christian schools are in fierce competition with their own church's youth ministry. It is important that both the philosophy of the Christian day school ministry and the youth ministry coincide. They should maintain the same Bible standards on separation, modesty in dress, hair length for boys, Bible doctrine, and rules for youth and school activities. I am afraid in many cases we defeat our own young people because of inconsistencies in leadership.

The youth director has the distinct advantage of not being on the "inside" of the school. The school is not primarily his responsibility or ministry. This enables him to be more effective in counseling since the young people are able to confide in him without fear of disciplinary action. It is for this reason that I believe it extremely difficult for a youth director to be a teacher also. When a teen is to receive assignments, grades and discipline from his teacher, it is hard for him to be open if the same man is also his youth director.

Overemphasis on sports is a danger in a Christian school. The most pleasing thing to the Lord is not how many touchdowns a boy makes, but how many souls he wins and how consistent he is in his walk with the Lord. This is why it is extremely important that the youth ministry and Christian school possess the same philosophy in regard to what they are trying to accomplish in the lives of youth.

6 — Preaching to Teens

Many adults mistakenly believe that young people will not respond to the preaching of the Word of God. On the contrary, I have found that the teenager is waiting to be told the truth. Even the most rebellious young person will acknowledge that he has heard the truth when the Bible is preached. It is the Word of God which chisels away the hardness in a young person's life.

I have repeatedly told parents, "I am no miracle man. I cannot make your young person do right, neither can I change his life. Only God can do that. And this is accomplished through the preaching of the Word."

There are no shortcuts to reaching teens. God's plan is the only plan which will succeed, and He tells us that it is the Word which will bring about saving faith. It is the Word which cleanses a person's life, be he young or old, teen or adult. The young people's problems are answered for them in the Word of God. It is the most current and relevant Book one could ever use in dealing with teenagers.

Because preaching is the plan ordained by God to reach teenagers, the one delivering the message must have certain qualifications. When a man preaches, it is absolutely necessary that he have a burden for those to whom he preaches. He must know what it is to weep out of a heart of compassion and concern over the sin and folly which destroys the lives of our youth.

When I invite a speaker to preach to my teens, I make certain that he has a heart for teenagers. Many good preachers just do not have the compassion and love for young people that is vital if they are to reach them. Those preachers are better off preaching to another age group.

Sometimes youth workers think they must be young in order to effectively preach and minister to youth. I abhor the concept that a man must look and act like teenagers in order to have rapport with them. Teenagers need a leader, not an imitator. Some of the best preachers that I have invited to speak to my young people have been mature men who have a heart for teens, yet are willing to be the leaders and preach the Word of God in a straight way. The most ludicrous thing I know of is an adult dressing or acting like a teen when he is beyond those years.

This does not detract from the fact that a youth preacher must be young at heart. He should combine the joy of living with a maturity which will allow him to minister effectively to teens.

One who desires to preach to young people must be prepared before he enters the pulpit. A man who attempts to preach to teenagers in the power of the flesh is a fool. Fresh, Spirit-anointed preaching is the only kind that can bring conviction to the heart and changes in the life. If I did not know that the Holy Spirit would fill and use me, I would never again stand to preach to young people. God will not use a dirty vessel which has not been emptied of self. Therefore, it is vital that the preacher be cleansed and anointed by the Spirit, or his words will be vain babblings which will accomplish nothing for God.

A preacher must have the right attitude toward preaching and believe that he is doing the will of God. If he is to have success, he must also have a God-given burden and love for those to whom he ministers. He must be a student of the Bible and spend time "searching the scriptures" for the truths of God. Each message must be bathed in prayer.

A preacher should have the basic thoughts of the sermon in mind several days before he delivers it, thus allowing him time to meditate upon his subject. He should develop the subject first in his own mind, then refine it on paper before delivering it to the audience.

It is important that a servant of God be prepared to preach at any and all times. A preacher should never refuse a preaching opportunity unless he has a conflict. Therefore, it is important that he develop many messages in order to be constantly prepared.

Many youth leaders have told me that they do not know what materials or ideas to use in preaching to young people. Let me point you to an inexhaustible sourcebook which deals with the issues of life—the Bible.

In choosing topics, one must select subjects which are relevant to the teenage audience. The topic needs to be interesting and must be pertinent to their needs. Some suggestions are listed below.

1. Obedience to parents
2. Getting along with people.
   a. hatred
   b. bitterness
   c. gossip
   d. jealousy
   e. strife
   f. division
3. Faithfulness
   a. to the Lord
   b. to the church
   c. to the youth group
   d. to the youth pastor
4. Need for Bible reading
5. Soul winning
6. Evils of the day
   a. music
   b. drugs
   c. television
   d. movies
   e. drinking
   f. smoking
7. Bible doctrines
8. Rebellion
9. Dating relationships
10. Attitudes
11. Goals
12. Character

13. Love
14. Philosophy of the world (Col. 2:8)
15. Burdens

From the above list of suggestions, a youth preacher could prepare several messages to help the teenager in his Christian life.

A preacher should be scriptural in his presentation. Scripture verses should also be used to prove points. The Bible should be made to live, and teenagers should be encouraged to bring their own Bibles.

Illustrations are invaluable to the preacher because they help make the points clear and allow the teens to understand more easily. They provide the needed tools for driving the truth home to the heart and help keep the attention of the audience.

Good illustrations can be obtained from the Bible, from personal experiences, and from news articles. I suggest you never select illustrations from the lives of members of the youth group. Be certain that the illustrations are relevant to the topic and are an asset to the message.

Not only is the message of prime importance, but the manner in which it is delivered should also be of special concern. I have been accused of being too hard on our teenagers, but teenagers like to hear it "straight." Christ was against sin and made it hard for people to remain neutral, and we should pattern our preaching after Him. Young people have been told and shown the wrong way to live by the world, and it is the preacher's duty to lift up his voice and declare the right way as revealed in the Word of God.

Therefore, a preacher must preach with power. He must be willing to preach the truth without fear of being intimidated by the teen. He must take careful aim in his preaching and be certain to hit the target. Many times he must demand their attention. This can be accomplished by having good subject material, by not letting the service drag, and by not prolonging the service too long. Occasionally a preacher must speak out with authority to the teens who would disturb the service by talking or laughing.

Preachers must be careful to be themselves, not try to copy others. Every technique or method used by the preacher in presenting the message should be overshadowed and permeated with the compassion and concern he has for each teen in the audience.

I have found that many times a point can be driven home to the heart by the telling of humorous incidents. These stories, when linked to the Word of God, will bring conviction.

May youth preachers strive to deliver the message of God in such a way as to reach the hearts of needy young people.

A preacher who has a Spirit-filled life, is prepared, has God's message, and skillfully but forcefully delivers that message, may expect certain results. He may expect the Holy Spirit to bring conviction in hearts, causing teens to respond by trusting Christ. There may be a change in the attitudes, lifestyle and service of the teens. The youth group will begin to grow and should become spiritually stronger as each grows in his spiritual life.

In summary let me reiterate: teenagers need strong Bible preaching in order to live successful Christian lives. Let us be willing to put forth the effort and dedication necessary in order to help our teens, both individually and as a group, grow spiritually and learn the right way to conduct their lives.

7 — Camps and Retreats

We have a unique situation at Trinity Baptist Church because we have our own church-owned camp. In directing the teenage weeks of camp, I have seen the Lord bless the work because we have maintained discipline and high Bible standards.

In some camps the emphasis is placed upon sports, activities, music, counselors, and the personnel. However, a youth camp should be built around *preaching*. As I have stated before in chapter 6, the teenager who is reached for Christ is touched by Spirit-filled preaching that reveals sin and uplifts Jesus Christ. A camper soon learns what is the most important aspect of camp life. And it is amazing to see even unsaved ones look with respect to the preaching time and upon the preachers.

Gear the services and classroom sessions to edify, train and reinforce Bible standards and teachings. Build the camping program itself around the speaker. Thus, it is very important that the best speaker available be obtained for their week of camp.

As has been stated many times before, **"Idle hands are the Devil's workshop."** Therefore, keep the teenager involved in activities at all times. Even when space is limited, organized activities can be a real highlight of the camp.

The activities should involve team competition. Place each teenager on a team, and involve as many as possible.

Make the activities wholesome and exciting. The competition between teams should earn points for the winners, and the excitement should build until the final day when the campers leave. Include memorizing of Scripture and encourage each camper to learn the Word of God.

At the end of the week, recognize one winner. Give awards to the boy and girl camper of the week, to the boy and girl who memorized the most Scripture, and to the winning team. Make the week's activities thrilling for each young person.

Many youth leaders think that one cannot reach unsaved young people with the Gospel if Bible standards on dress are maintained. We have seen just the opposite at our camp. It is important that the leaders have a strong philosophy as to standards. However, having convictions is not enough; they must be consistently enforced. Publish a rule sheet so that everyone is aware of what is expected of him or her. The rules should encourage boys to be men and girls to be ladies. It is extremely important that the rules not promote love affairs and not allow young people to be together alone.

The teenage camp counselor needs to be saved. Second, he should be abiding in Christ and in fellowship with the Lord. The counselors play an important role in any camp's success. It is their opportunity to have a close, personal interest in each camper assigned to them. What an opportunity to win lost teens to the Lord!

At our camp, few on the camp staff are paid. The majority of our counselors are volunteers from our church and other Bible-preaching churches. Therefore, it is essential that they are screened by the camp director and given instructions on dealing with teenagers.

Not everyone has the disposition to work with a teenager. Therefore, it is essential that a counselor have genuine love for and understanding of teenagers. Fourth, a counselor needs to know how to obey an order himself before he or she can ever expect a teenager to obey orders. Fifth, a camp counselor needs to be loyal to the camp director and to the goals desired to be accomplished in the young person's life. Never should a counselor disagree with the camp director or camp rules in the presence of a teenager.

A camping program which is based primarily on Bible preaching, is centered around the preacher, involves the young people in good, exciting activities and enforces standards can and will be blessed by God. Many lives will be touched for the Lord. Many young people will make lasting and important decisions which will change the entire course and destiny of their lives.

SENIOR HIGH SCHEDULE OF EVENTS

August 6 - 11, 1979

MONDAY

11:00 a.m.	Registration	6:00	Dinner
1:00	Lunch	6:30-7:00	Funspiration top of hill
1:30	Girls load bus for swimming	7:10-7:40	Bible Quiz at tabernacle
1:45-3:00	Girls swim time; Boys jet ski	7:45	Evening service
2:00	Boys canteen	9:15	Canteen
3:00	Boys load bus for swimming	9:45	Team competition
3:15-5:00	Boys swim time	10:30	Prepare for bed
3:45	Girls canteen, jet ski	10:50	Devotions
4:15-5:00	Girls recreation or memory work	11:00	Lights out!.

TUESDAY

7:00 a.m.	Rise and shine	2:00	Boys canteen
7:15	Morning devotions	3:00	Boys load for swimming
7:30	Flag salute	3:15-5:00	Boys swim time
7:35-8:00	Start on cabin clean-up	3:45	Girls canteen, jet ski
8:00	Breakfast	4:15-5:00	Girls recreation or memory work
8:30	Cabin clean-up		
9:00-9:55	Bible class-Dr. Terry Smith	6:00	Dinner
10:00-10:20	Team competition top of hill	6:30-7:00	Funspiration top of hill
10:35-11:10	All girls' class--Mrs. Nancy Reilly (boys' recreation)	7:10-7:40	Bible Quiz
11:15-11:40	Canteen	7:45	Evening service
11:45-12:25	Bible class--Dr. Ron Reilly	9:15	Canteen
12:30	Lunch	9:45	Team competition
1:30	Girls load for swimming	10:30	Prepare for bed
1:45-3:00	Girls swim time (boys recreation, jet ski	10:50	Devotions
		11:00	Lights out!

WEDNESDAY

7:00 a.m.	Rise and shine	2:00	Boys canteen
7:15	Morning devotions	3:00	Boys load for swimming
7:30	Flag salute	3:15-5:00	Boys swim time
7:35	Start cabin clean-up	3:45	Girls canteen, jet ski
8:00	Breakfast	4:15-5:00	Girls recreation and memory work
8:30	Cabin clean-up		
9:00-9:55	Bible class--Dr. Terry Smith	6:00	Dinner
10:00-10:20	Team competition top of hill	6:30-7:00	Funspiration top of hill
10:25-11:10	All boys class--Dr. Terry Smith (girls recreation)	7:10-7:40	Bible Quiz
11:15-11:40	Canteen	7:45	Evening service
11:45-12:25	Bible class--Dr. Ron Reilly	9:15	Canteen
12:30	Lunch	9:45	Team competition
1:30	Girls load for swimming	10:30	Prepare for bed
1:45-3:00	Girls swim time (boys recreation jet ski)	10:50	Devotions
		11:00	Lights out!

THURSDAY

7:00 a.m.	Rise and shine	2:00	Canteen
7:15	Morning devotions	3:00	Boys load bus for swim
7:30	Flag salute	3:15-5:00	Boys swim time
7:35	Start cabin clean-up	3:45	Girls canteen, jet ski
8:00	Breakfast	4:15-5:00	Girls recreation &
8:30	Cabin clean-up		memory work
9:00-9:55	Bible class--Dr. Terry Smith	6:00	Dinner
10:00-10:20	Team competition top of hill	6:30-7:00	Funspiration top of hill
10:25-11:10	All Girls class--Mrs. Nancy	7:10-7:40	Bible Quiz
	Reilly (boys recreation)	7:45	Evening service
11:15-11:40	Canteen	9:15	Canteen
11:45-12:25	Bible class--Dr. Ron Reilly	9:45	Team competition
12:30	Lunch	10:30	Prepare for bed
1:30	Girls load bus for swimming	10:50	Devotions
1:45-3:00	Girls swim time	11:00	Lights out!
	(boys recreation, jet ski)		

FRIDAY

7:00	Rise and shine	12:15	Lunch
7:15	Morning devotions	12:45	WAR
7:30	Flag salute	2:30-3:45	Girls swim time
7:35	Start cabin clean-up		(boys recreation, jet ski)
8:00	Breakfast	4:00-5:30	Boys swim time
8:30	Cabin clean-up		(girls jet ski, canteen)
8:50-9:45	Bible class--Dr. Terry Smith	6:15	Dinner
9:45-9:55	Break	6:45	Funspiration
10:00-10:40	All Boys class--Dr. Smith	7:25-7:55	Bible Quiz
	(girls recreation)	8:00	Evening service
10:45-11:05	Canteen	9:30	Canteen
11:10-11:50	Bible class--Dr. Ron Reilly	10:00	Presentation of Awards
11:50	Instructions for WAR	11:00	Lights out!

TRINITY YOUTH CAMP

DATES_____

NAME	REG. FEE	BALANCE	CABIN	BED

8 — Banquets

Each year the youth group of Trinity Baptist Church provides an annual teen banquet for all the church young people, the Christian high school students, and any guests of the teens. The objectives of this banquet are as follows:

I. TO PROVIDE AN OPPORTUNITY FOR YOUNG PEOPLE TO SOCIALIZE IN A CHRISTIAN ATMOSPHERE.
   A. Does not copy the world.
   B. Does not provide worldly entertainment.
      1. Does not provide long, out-of-place skits.
      2. Does not provide the wrong type of music.
      3. Requires modest and proper standards of dress.
      4. Provides a Christian atmosphere—a first-class banquet.

II. TO PROVIDE A DISCIPLINED CHRISTIAN-CONTROLLED ATMOSPHERE.
   A. Does provide a good time.
   B. Does provide good character-building activities.

III. TO RECOGNIZE THE SPIRITUAL ACCOMPLISHMENTS OF TEENAGERS OVER THE PAST YEAR.
   A. Does provide a review of the highlights of the year's activities.
   B. Does encourage other young people to mature and grow in the Lord.

IV. TO PROVIDE AN ANTICIPATED ACTIVITY FOR THE TEENS EVERY YEAR.
   A. Provides one major banquet per year.

B. Provides an occasion for dating, but it is not mandatory or encouraged by the leader.

If a banquet is to be successful, it must be planned carefully.

I. THE BANQUET REQUIRES A GENERAL THEME.
A. The theme must be chosen after careful study and thought.
B. The theme must be visualized as to how it would appear in the banquet area.
C. The theme can sometimes be given a title which conveys the theme.
D. The theme should be different and unusual.
   1. The effort involved will bring dividends.
   2. Visitors will be impressed by the uniqueness of the theme.

II. THE BANQUET REQUIRES A SPEAKER.
A. The speaker must have good rapport with young people.
B. The speaker may have special qualifications.
   1. He may be an "outstanding" preacher.
   2. He may be an "outstanding" athlete.
C. The speaker must be a dedicated, separated Christian.
D. The speaker must be chosen several months in advance.

The location of the banquet is also very important, and the choice should be made after the following are considered:

1. The place should be large enough to accommodate a possible overflow.
2. The banquet should take place in a reputable establishment.
3. The establishment should provide good food.
4. The location should be easily accessible.
5. The facilities should be able to provide a platform, a PA system, and a piano.
6. The site should be chosen well in advance of the banquet—from six months to a year.

7. The banquet will be more successful if it is held in a location other than the church building.

In order to provide the best possible food, the following guidelines should be observed:

1. Serve "buffet style" in order to conserve time.
2. Two or three choices from each of the major food divisions should be provided.(Example: two meats, two vegetables, two desserts.)
3. The amount of food should be carefully selected and care taken to ensure a sufficient amount before the guests arrive.
4. The cost must be kept within reason, but at the same time must provide an outstanding occasion for the teens.

The theme of the banquet should be broad enough to ensure its usefulness and workability. Before selecting a theme, all aspects should be considered. Do not fear to select a topic which would involve the spending of money and time. The theme should be selected at least seven months in advance and work should begin five months before the banquet.

The following is a list of suggested ideas for possible themes:

1. Bicentennial
2. Old-time Ice Cream Parlor
3. Disney World
4. Knight of Nights
5. Candyland

The decorations can greatly add to the atmosphere and can help "set the mood" for the occasion. The four main areas which need to be decorated are as follows:

1. Displays should me made for each table.
   a. Colorful, but not gaudy.
   b. Simple, but unusual.
   c. Small, but not microscopic.
   d. Some possible suggestions are as follows:

  (1) Small painting easels for a French theme
  (2) Small Mickey Mouse ears (hat) for a Disney World theme.
  (3) Small tulips made from egg cartons for a spring theme.
2. Decorate the entrance to the banquet room.
  a. Place theme title in the entrance.
  b. The entrance decorations should be appealing to the eye and correspond with the theme.
  c. The entrance decorations should not cause congestions and hinder those who serve the food.
3. Decorate the banquet room as follows:
  a. An enlarged replica to follow the theme. (For example, if the theme is an "Old-Fashioned Ice Cream Parlor," perhaps an enlarged banana split.)
  b. Don't overcrowd because of decorations.
  c. The objects which are already present within the room should be included within the theme.
4. Make area designated for the taking of pictures especially attractive.
  a. Decorations should follow the banquet theme.
  b. Decorations should appear lifelike and be very colorful. (Living, potted plants can be obtained as a background for taking pictures.)
  c. Obtain a good photographer who will take good pictures at inexpensive rates.
  d. This area should be in operation before and after the banquet in order to generate business.
  e. Pictures will allow young people to remember the occasion.

In order for the banquet to be a success, it is important that committees be established.

1. Appoint an "idea" committee to choose proper decorations.
  a. Let it be made up of young people actively involved in the youth ministry.

    b. Choose the best logical decorations.

    c. The chosen theme should be supported by the committee.

2. Choose a "promotion" committee to advertise and promote the activity.

    a. This committee should design and produce attractive posters. Provide an occasional skit in the Sunday morning service to promote the banquet.

    b. Procure and distribute fliers.

    c. Stress "word-of-mouth" advertisement.

3. Establish a "work" committee composed mainly of teenagers.

    a. This committee should provide an opportunity for many young people to participate in setting up and decorating.

    b. Schedule work activities so there will be no conflicts with other group meetings.

    c. Give definite assignments to each member of this committee.

4. A "clean-up" committee is so important.

    a. Choose special young people for this committee.

    b. Remove all decorations immediately after the banquet.

    c. Handle carefully all decorations for future use.

    d. Obtain in advance necessary vehicles for removing decorations and equipment.

5. Appoint an "appreciation" committee which will officially offer "thank you's" for all who helped with or participated in the banquet.

    a. This committee may convey expressions of appreciation by "word of mouth."

    b. A personal "thank you" to each person who had a part. (This personal contact means a great deal to all who work so faithfully!)

The program itself should deal with three areas—the order, the speaker and the awards.

The *order* of the program should be printed on beautifully designed programs which state the sequence of events as well as the food being served. The programs should be consistent with the banquet theme. The events of the evening should move smoothly and swiftly from one event to the other.

The *speaker* should not be hindered by a time limit, since the message is the most important part of the banquet. Don't hinder him with long, drawn-out preliminaries which can sometimes "make or break" the entire banquet.

The speaker should be provided for financially with travel expenses and an honorarium. In addition, housing and transportation to and from the banquet should be supplied. Remember, he is your "honored" guest.

Present several awards during the banquet. Our teenagers who participate in the Daytona soul-winning trip are given an award. Athletes in the secular world receive awards for winning, so why shouldn't Christians be rewarded for their merits in soul winning? Each trophy is engraved with the teen's name, number of souls he personally won to the Lord, and the total won by the entire group. Perhaps this could be carried over to churches who have outstanding soul-winning teenagers.

Those who chaperone the teens during the Daytona trip are given a plaque displaying their team's accomplishments. Chaperones for church youth groups could receive some recognition similar to this.

A large trophy, kept by the youth department, is used to honor the team chosen as the group best exemplifying the Lord in their soul winning, their Christian character and their attitude while witnessing at Daytona. A plate is engraved with the name of that group and remains on display throughout the year. We replace the plate each year with a similar plate bearing the name of the current group winners.

Christian Character awards are presented to a boy and girl senior who have proven throughout the years that they have been involved in the youth ministry. This award is given on the basis of faithfulness, character, attitude and spiritual stamina. The following is a list of nine different categories by which the nominees are measured:

1. Integrity
2. Faithfulness to:
   a. the Lord
   b. the church
   c. youth activities
   d. youth director
3. Loyalty to:
   a. the Lord
   b. the church
   c. the youth group
   d. the youth director
4. Separation:
   a. unto the Lord
   b. apart from the world
5. Testimony:
   a. church
   b. school
   c. home
6. Appearance:
   a. modesty
   b. cleanliness
   c. hair
7. Dependability:
   a. can be depended on for everything
   b. punctual
8. Convictions:
   a. have developed convictions from the Bible
   b. are not ashamed to express them in a spiritual manner
9. Friendliness

The recipients of the Christian Character Award are selected by the Guard of Honor one month prior to the banquet, and the winners announced the night of the banquet.

A medal is given to any young person in the youth group who has been able to enlist teens into the youth group throughout the year. The recruits must exhibit a personal interest in the youth ministry, must be faithful to activities and services, must make a public profession, and must develop a spiritual outlook toward others, toward the Word of God and toward the problems which they confront.

An important phase of the program is the special music. This should be provided by special groups or individuals within the youth group. Contact the young people at least two months in advance. They should be willing to do their best by putting in the necessary practice. Singers must be properly and modestly attired and the boys' hair cut in a man's style and length.

Seniors and their dates are recognized during the banquet. They are given free tickets to the event and are seated in a special section of the banquet room, near the speaker's platform.

Gear the message to reach the lost and challenge the Christians. It is imperative that an invitation be given.

A youth banquet can be a memorable and spiritual highlight for your young people if it is well planned and organized.

Cover

Inside Menu

La Carte
MENU
hors d'oeuvres
relish tray

rôti de boeuf : crevette Newburgh : jambon glacé
roast beef : shrimp Newburg : glazed smoked ham

petits haricots verts aux carottes
tiny green beans with carrots
pommes de terre : salade verte
oven brown potatoes : tossed green salad

tarte aux cerises   ou   pudding de banane
cherry pie   or   banana pudding

petit pain frais : café ou thé
fresh baked rolls : coffee or tea

"*Palatable Foods*"

Ambassadors for Christ
10th Annual Teen Banquet

Invocation -------------------- Steve Hollenbeck

• *Dinner* •

Greeting of Guests ------------- Rev. Ron Reilly
• Presentation of Awards
• Daytona Soulwinning
• Christian Character

Introduction of Speaker

Special Music --- Ambassadors for Christ Chorale

Message ------------ Dr. Ken Hay

Benediction ----- Dr. Bob Gray

Fine

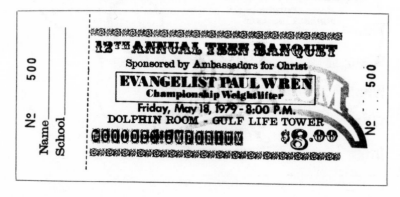

6th ANNUAL TEEN BANQUET

Ambassadors for Christ

SPEAKER: LEE (ROCK) BOYER
Football Coach of U.S. Navy Academy

FRIDAY, MAY 18, 1973 — 8:00 P.M.

PROMENADE ROOM — HILTON HOTEL

№ 654   Price $4.50

№ 654

Name
School

№ 350

№ 350

Name
School

11th Annual Teen Banquet

Sponsored by Ambassadors for Christ

Speaker: Dr. Terry ____

Pastor, Longview, Texas

Monday, May 29, 1978 - 7:00 P.M.

DOLPHIN ROOM - GULF LIFE BUILDING

№ 350   Price: $7.50

THEME: **WALT DISNEY'S MAGIC KINGDOM**

№ 500

№ 500

№ 500

Name
School

12TH ANNUAL TEEN BANQUET

Sponsored by **Ambassadors for Christ**

EVANGELIST PAUL WREN
Championship Weight lifter

Friday, May 18, 1979 - 8:00 P.M.

DOLPHIN ROOM - GULF LIFE TOWER

GEORGIA EMPORIUM   **$8.00**

Where • Dolphin Room - Gulf Life Tower

When • Friday, May 20 at 8 p.m.

Who • All Teenagers, Grades 7-12

What • Fantastic Program - All You Can Eat - $7.00

Dress • Formal or Semi-Formal - For Tickets Contact Bro. Reilly - 786-5320

Ambassadors for Christ

Front

12TH ANNUAL
TEEN BANQUET

THE MENU

FROM THE KITCHEN

1 OLD-TYME PLATE
Roast Round of Beef

2 DELICIOUS SHRIMP FANTASY
Shrimp Creole with Rice

3 ALL AMERICAN PLATTER
Fried Chicken

FROM THE SALAD BAR

1 Assorted Relish Trays
2 Tossed Salad

ON THE SIDE

1 Parsley & New Potatoes
2 Green Bean Almondine
3 Glazed Carrots

DESSERTS

1 Strawberry Shortcake
2 Cherry Cobbler

AND ETC...

**Fresh Rolls   Coffee
Tea**

THE PROGRAM

Invocation
MIKE BUTLER

Dinner

Greeting of Guests
DR. RON REILLY

Presentation of Awards
BIBLE CLUB OF THE YEAR
DAYTONA SOULWINNING
CHRISTIAN CHARACTER

Introduction of Speaker

Special Music
AMBASSADORS FOR CHRIST
ENSEMBLE

Message
EVANGLIST PAUL WRENN

Benediction
DR. BOB GRAY

COMPLIMENTS

MUSIC	SURREY & BONESHAKER
MR. WINSTON MILLER	LAKESHORE SCHWINN CYCLERY
NICE HOUSE OF MUSIC	2108 Blanding Blvd.
Roosevelt Mall	

THE GOLDEN EMPORIUM

Back

TWELFTH EDITION — JACKSONVILLE, FLORIDA — FRIDAY, MAY 18, 1979

Thursday, Friday, Saturday

The White House — MAX·KALISKI

Thursday, Friday, Saturday

SUPERB MILLINERY OPENING EVENT.

THURSDAY, Friday and Saturday we unveil the millinery splendor of the Old World and the New in a gorgeous gathering of modistes beauty and magnificence. London, Berlin and those brilliant stars of the Paris galaxy contribute their quota of superelegant creations. There is a copious showing of American models and copies; and not least, the interfelials productions of our own artists, which do not suffer by comparison with the originations of more renowned designers.

YOU ARE INVITED TO VIEW THIS EXALTED EXHIBITION.

Cover

Inside Menu

Ambassadors for Christ
11th Annual Teen Banquet

INVOCATION
Robert Lee

DINNER

GREETING OF GUESTS
Dr. Ron Reilly

PRESENTATION OF AWARDS
BIBLE CLUB OF THE YEAR
DAYTONA SOULWINNING
CHRISTIAN CHARACTER

INTRODUCTION OF SPEAKER

SPECIAL MUSIC
Ambassadors for Christ Chorale

MESSAGE
Dr. Terry Smith

BENEDICTION
Dr. Ron Reilly

From the Dining Car

SALADS

ENGINEER'S FAVORITE
(Tossed Salad)
BOILERMAN'S BOWL
(Waldorf Salad)

ENTREES

CONDUCTOR'S SPECIAL
Steamship Round of Roast Beef
BRAKEMAN'S DELIGHT
Southern Fried Chicken
STATION MASTER'S PLATE
Shrimp Creole with Rice

VEGETABLES

STEWARD'S DISH   PULLMAN'S ORDER
Oven Brown Potatoes   Glazed Fresh Carrots
AGENT'S BAKE
Baked Squash

DESSERTS

MICKEY MOUSE'S BIRTHDAY CAKE
GOOFY'S TREAT Bread Pudding with Orange Sauce
CLARABELLE'S SURPRISE Strawberry Shortcake
FRESH ROLLS   COFFEE OR TEA

MAGIC KINGDOM R.R.

11th Annual Teen Banquet 1978

9 — Hindrances to the Youth Ministry

It is the desire of Satan to hinder the teenager in his walk with the Lord by whatever means he can.

Ephesians 6:1-4 states:

"Children obey your parents in the Lord: for this is right. Honour thy father and mother; which is the first commandment with promise; that it may be well with thee, and thou mayest live long on the earth. And, ye fathers, provoke not your children to wrath: but bring them up in the nurture and admonition of the Lord."

This is a twofold commandment from the Lord. For years I have admonished teenagers to honor and obey their parents. The one who does so is promised by the Lord long life on this earth. However, the heartbreak of my ministry has been parents not willing to surrender their children to serve the Lord. Many of these parents, of course, are unsaved and so cannot be expected to understand spiritual truths; but the sad fact is that many *Christian* parents hinder their young folk from being used of God.

Parents may hinder their children in the following ways:

1. Discipline the teen by keeping him from a youth activity or visitation.
2. Criticize the youth programs in the presence of the children.
3. Criticize the youth director or pastor in the child's presence.
4. Complain about the cost of activities. (They may give money freely for other activities such as athletics, clothes, or school.)

5. Allow their teenager to attend worldly activities such as movies and rock concerts.
6. Neglect to have family devotions on a consistent basis.
7. Fail to encourage their young people to have their own, personal devotions.
8. Have more physical and material goals than spiritual goals for their teens.
9. Allow a "double standard" in the home.
10. Permit their teenagers to work rather than insisting they attend church and become involved in the youth activities.

Youth director, it is your responsibility to help parents understand the purpose of the youth group in order to gain their support and concern. You may accomplish this goal by means of the following:

1. Visit the home.
2. Invite the parents to assist with teenage activities and visitation by being chaperones.
3. With the pastor, promote the youth group and activities from the pulpit.
4. Write a personal letter to the parents expressing the purpose of the youth group and your desire to work with the family's teens.
5. Publicly advertise the victories which are results of the teenagers' soul-winning efforts.
6. Allow some of the young people to give personal testimonies of special victories.
7. Publish regular reports in a newsletter or bulletin.

A second hindrance to the youth ministry is sports, which can become a god to teenagers and can cause them to not serve the Lord during their teen years. A youth director must constantly remind the teenagers not to make sports the most important thing or they will become a "drop" out in the Lord's service.

Many times a job can be the downfall of a once faithful young person. Give a teenager responsibilities, but don't let these responsibilities interfere with the teen's church attendance and service, or it will harm him spiritually. It can also give the teenager a spirit of independence and cause him to feel he does not need anyone and, as a result, does not want any help spiritually.

"Rebellion is as the sin of witchcraft." This is often what causes a teenager to isolate himself from anything spiritual. This, of course, is a heart problem, and only the Holy Spirit can break the spirit of rebellion that rules in many lives. Parents, keep the teen under the preaching of the Word of God so that God's Spirit can penetrate the rebellious heart.

The teenager's friends are very important, and they can have a great influence on his future. Youth directors and parents must join forces in order to guide the teenager in choosing his friends. Parents, don't fear to break up wrong friendships but insist that your son or daughter choose the right companions. First Corinthians 15:33 says, "Evil communications corrupt good manners." A teenager from a good Christian home and with good morals can be ruined by the influence of one bad friend. It is very important that the teenager participate in a good youth group which will keep him involved in the right kind of activities and with the right kind of young people influencing his decisions and beliefs.

Dating can be a hindrance to the youth ministry, so teach your young people not to date the unsaved. The Bible plainly teaches in II Corinthians 6:14, "Be ye not unequally yoked together with unbelievers: for what fellowship hath righteousness with unrighteousness? and what communion hath light with darkness?" God has clearly stated that teenagers are not to have fellowship or communion with unbelievers.

When the Christian teen dates an unsaved person, he is out of the will of God and will soon be out of the Lord's service. In the years that I have been at Trinity, I have never seen a saved young person date an unsaved teen who did not hinder his life spiritually. So we must teach our young people to date only good Christian teenagers so their lives will count for God.

Carnal-minded Christian teens who date other teens in the

youth group will have a detrimental effect upon the group, working against everything the youth leader is attempting to do. Carnal young people are interested in their social and physical relationships, so they will "pull down" those who are striving to serve the Lord. For these reasons, it is important that youth activities never be promoted as "dating activities."

There is nothing wrong with a boy and girl having a good Christian relationship if Jesus Christ comes first; but when He is not put in His proper place and when the teens exclude themselves from everyone else, then the relationship is a hindrance to the unity of the group.

We have tried to build this unity within the youth group by not planning activities which will allow the dating couples to be alone and by preventing the couples from being partners in any of the activities. This allows the young people to meet and know other teens and thus helps to promote a unified group of teenagers who as one are striving to serve the Lord.

Most teenagers are "hung up" on the music of this day, and this in itself could be the biggest hindrance to the youth ministry. If the teens listen to worldly music, their philosophy will be wrong, their ability to think correctly will be hindered, and their actions will be, sooner or later, as worldly as the music they hear.

So, youth director, it is important that you help them get victory over listening to rock music by teaching them what the right kind of music is. If possible, tell the parents the evils of the wrong kind of music and its power to destroy their children. Teenagers who listen to rock music will never be what they can be for the Lord, and their lives can be completely ruined if they are not taught how to get victory.

It is very difficult to work with a teenager who has a "bad attitude." Not only is the young person hindering his own life, but he is spreading his attitude to others, causing them to also have bad attitudes.

The only way to help such a person is to pray for him, to talk with him about his problem, and to keep him actively involved in youth activities.

You youth workers must realize that there will be many hindrances in working with teens, and you must be able to recognize these hindrances and effectively deal with each.

10 — Characteristics of Teens

Today, many teenagers are walking in the wrong path and are not honoring the Lord. Instead, they are demonstrating those characteristics which, most certainly, will "lead to destruction" and to a ruined life.

One of those characteristics is that of "apathy." A "don't-care" attitude causes deadness and carelessness. It is very difficult to motivate such people. Soul winning means nothing to them; activities produce no excitement; they do not want to be spiritually minded. Of course, this apathetic attitude easily influences other teens; so a youth leader must warn his young people of the dangers of this "don't-care" attitude.

Another characteristic so prevalent in teenagers is disrespect and disregard for authority and spiritual leadership. Disrespect can cause great harm to the youth ministry. These teenagers usually pit parents against youth director. It is very important that these young people be taught the Word of God.

Hebrews 3:17 and I Thessalonians 5:12,13 plainly teach respect for spiritual leaders. It is imperative that the pastor support the youth leader.

A common characteristic of most teenagers is "love of the world" (II Tim. 4:10). All of the young people with whom I have worked have had to battle love of the world. Satan uses its allurements to tempt teenagers to leave the Lord out of their lives. The sad truth is that many do fall into the Devil's snare and fail to live for Christ. A youth director must deal with this problem in his preaching and teaching and at the same time be careful not "to turn them off" from hearing him. He must constantly remind them that the Devil uses rock music, television, unsaved friends, and sometimes unsaved parents, to destroy their lives.

A teenager who begins with the Lord, progresses to a certain point, then continues no further, illustrates the characteristic of "incomplete obedience." He may become involved in the youth group and may even become a soul winner, but he will not fully obey the Lord in the matter of separation or heeding the commands of the Bible. These young people should fear having their lives "messed up" because they are shallow and do not grow in the Lord.

A teenager who plays the role of a Christian but lives in sin and has no real love for the Lord is "deceitful." He not only deceives others, but deceives himself; therefore, he hurts others as well as himself. The youth pastor needs to preach on deception and expose deceit in the lives of young people.

A Christian teen who is in "complete rebellion" arrives at that condition after several seasons. He does not begin his Christian life filled with rebellion and a "hardened heart" (Prov. 29:1). Hebrews 3:7,8 states: "Wherefore as the Holy Ghost saith, To day if ye will hear his voice, Harden not your hearts, as in the provocation, in the day of temptation in the wilderness." Sometimes it seems the more truth a teenager hears, the harder he becomes. When this is the case, a pattern is being established which must be carefully avoided by all who would walk closely with the Lord. The pattern is as follows:

1. *Discontent.* The teen becomes dissatisfied with everything and everybody. Nothing "suits him." He criticizes everything and thinks he "knows it all."

2. *Self-centeredness.* He is the only one important. His parents no longer are important. The youth group is an afterthought. He cares only for himself—number one.

3. *Rebelliousness.* When the teen reaches this point in his life, the rebellion is very obvious both at home and at church. He gives everyone a "hard time." He does not realize to what extent his heart has become hardened.

4. *Destructiveness.* At this point, the teen does not care

about what happens to anything or anyone, including himself. He may destroy property or bring destruction upon people. He may even turn on his parents and physically try to harm them. He may come to the place of destroying his own body through drugs or other worldly vices.

5. *Unreachable.* This is a position that the teen reaches which forces the Lord to remove him from this world. It is necessary that you youth leaders do everything possible to reach this teen before he becomes unreachable. Parents, pastors, and youth leaders, don't be afraid to rebuke the teen before it is too late. Hebrews 3:13 says: "But exhort one another daily, while it is called To day; lest any of you be hardened through the deceitfulness of sin." Youth leaders do not preach and rebuke to bring harm to teens but to warn them and help them before God intervenes.

The characteristic of "popularity" means more to some teenagers than anything else in this world, yet it never brings peace or happiness. A Greek athlete once said, *"Fame is a vapor; popularity is an accident; money takes wings; the only thing that counts is* **character.***"* Many young people have wasted their lives by striving to get fame and popularity.

These seven characteristics, if allowed to rule and thrive, will "lead to destruction" and a wasted life.

11 — How Do You Measure a Successful Youth Ministry?

There are many differing opinions as to the meaning of "success." Throughout this book I have tried to convey that having big numbers in Sunday school or having gigantic activities for the young people does not necessarily mean success.

True success "shows up" when young people's lives have been built on the Word of God and soul winning. When young lives have been changed and God's Word has been allowed to mold the teen's character, then the youth director is able to begin seeing real fruit from his ministry.

The thrust of every youth ministry should be to help the teenagers find God's will. I have always sought to help young people set as one of their goals attending a Christian college after finishing high school.

Right motives now enter into the picture, and you youth directors must determine if you really care what happens to the teenager. If you are truly burdened for your teens, you will not be concerned about building the "greatest" youth group in America, but about building lives on the Word of God. You will want to see your teenagers get involved in soul winning throughout their teen years so they will know God's will upon graduating from high school

I believe that this best illustrates the scriptural approach to obtaining God's success. In Colossians 1:9 Paul states, "For this cause we also, since the day we heard it, do not cease to pray for you, and to desire that ye might be filled with the knowledge of *his will* in all wisdom and spiritual understanding." This verse plainly states that any Christian can know the will of God for his life. The Lord also promises to give spiritual wisdom so each can understand what is God's will for his life.

In realizing this truth, the question arises, "Why do so many young people miss God's will for their lives?" I believe the answer lies in the fact that they do not obey God's will during their teen years. What is the will of God for a teenager? Colossians 1:10 states, "That ye might walk worthy of the Lord unto all pleasing, being fruitful in every good work, and increasing in the knowledge of God."

These are three biblical truths that need to be activated in every teenager's life. In John 15:1-3 these three truths are revealed again:

"I am the true vine, and my Father is the husbandman. Every branch in me that beareth not fruit he taketh away: and every branch that beareth fruit, he purgeth it that it may bring forth more fruit." The main function of a Christian is to bear fruit, that is, to lead people to a saving knowledge of the Lord Jesus Christ. Soul winning is the key to any ministry for God, including the youth ministry. So in order to see young people go on for God, we must get them *involved* in soul winning.

A youth director wishing to be successful must put into practice three biblical principles.

The first is that of *separation* from the world. John 15:3 states, "Now ye are clean through the word that I have spoken unto you." Direct young people to cleanse the sin from their lives and "come out from among" the worldliness of this day. You can accomplish separation if you teach and preach the Bible and if you enforce rules and standards for all youth activities.

John 15:5 states, "I am the vine, ye are the branches: He that abideth in me, and I in him, the same bringeth forth much fruit: for without me ye can do nothing." This verse sets forth the importance of having unbroken *fellowship* with Christ. A Christian can be used to win many souls to Christ when there is nothing between him and the Lord. Teenagers who are in fellowship with the Lord will be happy, and the youth director will enjoy working with them.

During the Daytona trip in 1981, forty-six won 5,432 people to

Christ in three days. What a peace they had in their hearts, and what joy was expressed on their faces!

John 15:8 says, "Herein is my Father glorified, that ye bear much fruit." The third principle is that of bringing *glory* to God. A Christian can please the Lord by being a true witness and by bringing others into the kingdom of God. Many young people who attend church services or who are enrolled in Christian schools glibly state, "I love the Lord." However, this passage in John clearly shows that the way to really prove one's love for the Lord is to bring glory to Him by winning others.

John 15:16 needs to be put into practice in every youth group—"Ye have not chosen me, but I have chosen you, and ordained you, that ye should go and bring forth fruit, and that your fruit should remain: that whatsoever ye shall ask of the Father in my name, he may give it you."

Notice that it is *God's way:* He has chosen us to carry the message of His Son to the world. It is *God's Authority:* He has ordained us to tell others of their needs. It is *God's Method:* He desires that we go from "house to house" and into the "highways and hedges" to bring others to Christ. When we practice the above, we may expect *God's Results.*

Youth director, you need never be concerned about the size of your Sunday school department if you follow the plan revealed in John 15:16. The results will remain. If the teens are winning souls to Christ, some of the fruit is going to remain and the youth group will experience automatic growth.

As a result of employing this plan, we can say to the glory of God that many of our former teenagers, now adults, are serving the Lord faithfully. Thirty-three former youth group members are in full-time Christian service.

The proof of a successful youth ministry is not in what one has done, but in what his products are doing.

12 — Qualifications of a Successful Youth Director

I do not believe that just anyone should work with teenagers. In fact, there are many people who are involved in youth work who are not qualified and have no business being leaders of youth ministries. It is, therefore, important that you as a youth leader meet certain qualifications if you are to be used of God to build a solid youth department.

First, you must have an assurance of God's calling. You should know that God has called you to work specifically with youth. Working with teenagers is not a "glorified babysitting" position, nor should it be a "stepping stone" to the pastorate. The youth leader is responsible for the lives and futures of many teenagers, and God will not use a man to channel these teens if he has not been called of God to minister to them.

Second, if you are to help them grow spiritually, you must have a "burden" to reach young people with the Gospel. Some who work with teens do so with selfish motives. What is really needed are more leaders who have a God-given burden, and who are concerned with individual's lives and futures. A leader who has such a burden will love his teenagers, and they, in return, will love and respect him.

It is always difficult to work with teens since they are so unpredictable and subject to instability. A youth director who has a burdened heart will continue trying to help teens no matter how difficult the task becomes.

Third, you youth leaders must have "Bible standards" for your own lives and for those in the youth group. The teenagers will never be spiritual without Bible standards to live by. You must be the example for the teens, but you cannot expect them to live by standards unless you live by them yourself. Those standards should encompass every aspect of the youth ministry. On visitation, activities, or trips, boys should look like boys, and girls should appear as young ladies. The correct standards of dress will subdue open rebellion within the youth group.

Discipline is a part of standards but is neglected by so many youth directors. If teenagers are permitted to "do what they please," the result will always be trouble. Some churches and Christian schools have been embarrassed by open trouble with the public and the law because they have failed to promote proper leadership and to enforce discipline. To God's glory, Trinity Baptist Church is able to recall youth activities and trips of the past fourteen years with no embarrassment or shame. Standards prove to be successful when they are based upon Bible principles.

The fourth qualification is that you be a "man" and the "leader" of the youth ministry. Be a man of God whom the young people can respect and after whom they can pattern their lives. Never try to be a teenager in order to gain their acceptance. Be yourself and allow God to use you to help teens. Always keep the right relationship between boys and girls. Never touch the girls or allow them to touch you. Be careful to provide a good image of your family and the correct relationship between husband and wife. It is important that the wife of the youth leader be involved in the ministry and work by his side.

The fifth qualification is that you be a "preacher" of the Word of God. A leader must be able to preach if he is going to deal with the needs of youth. Preach the Word of God directly to the teenagers, not "at them."

The youth leader must be "flexible" and easy to work with. Be willing to adjust to any situation. On occasion, you may need to change a scheduled meeting at the pastor's request, and you should do so with a good spirit.

Finally, you, as a youth pastor, must be "stickable." Never leave a place of service in a church unless God so directs. Don't quit because the job is difficult or because you would rather work in some other place. Remember, you are trying to build the lives of young people. Lives cannot be built in two years, and yet that is the average length of time that a youth director remains in a church. In two years, the foundation has just been established, and real results will not be visible for at least five years.

Some churches have had two or three youth directors in two years' time. This is unhealthy for the church and harms the teenagers. It could hinder them from serving the Lord in future years. For almost fourteen years my wife and I served at Trinity Baptist Church; and we have seen many of our teenagers go out to serve as missionaries, pastors, youth directors, and Christian school teachers.

It is important for youth leaders to stay with the task in the place of God's calling and to determine not to quit for anything or anyone.

13 — Qualifications for Officers

Because young people are influenced by other teens and are constantly observing their lives, the following Covenant of Office and Standard of Conduct has been developed and must be accepted by all young people who are leaders and hold positions in the youth program of Trinity Baptist Church. It is a Bible-based standard and covenant. In order for the youth group to have the blessing of God, those who lead must be willing to maintain that testimony and to reap God's blessings in their own lives and to see other members of the youth group follow their examples. Thus, we have developed the following:

A COVENANT OF OFFICE AND STANDARD OF CONDUCT

I.   I believe the Bible is the only rule for faith and practice; therefore:

I will maintain a daily quiet time and "study to show /myself7 approved unto God."

I reject the philosophy of the "silent witness," and will endeavor to witness to some lost sinner each day, because "I am not ashamed of the Gospel of Christ."

II. I believe that the autonomous local church is the pillar and ground of the Truth and that Christianity as such has always been a "house," "book," religion; therefore:

I will be faithful in attendance at all worship services on Sunday and prayer meeting on Wednesday;

I will be faithful in attendance to the youth training union hour on Sunday night;

I will tithe my income;

I will be faithful in the teen visitation program and especially as it pertains to reaching young people through weekly activities paced by personal soul winning;

I will behave during all church services and will sit in an area designated for teens unless I am sitting with my parents, and I will encourage others to do likewise.

III.   I believe that Christ gave some "apostles; and some, prophets; and some, evangelists; and some, pastors and teachers; For the perfecting of the saints, for the work of the ministry, for the edifying of the body of Christ"; therefore:

I will obey them that have the rule over me and submit myself to their God-given authority;

I will give all loyalty to the pastoral and lay leadership of the Trinity Baptist Church;

I will not engage in criticism, gossip, or back-biting as regards leadership, nor will I stand in silence when this leadership is under attack but shall with all due courage and humility rebuke and reprove those who would sow seeds of discord among the brethren;

I will back the leadership of the youth director 100 percent: in obedience, conversation to him and in my behavior and attitude toward the youth ministry.

IV.   I believe that there should be no conflict between my secular life in school or at work and my church life; therefore:

I will schedule my time so that my church shall have precedence over my extra-curricular activities, and if legitimate conflict should arise, I shall give my church priority.

Youth activities will always have precedence over any school activity or job. There will be no exceptions. If providentially hindered, I will contact Brother Reilly beforehand. (Family is the only exception.)

V.   I believe that the Youth Group is a ministry of the New Testament local church and that the local church can only be scripturally comprised of born-again, baptized members; therefore:

I will do nothing as an elected officer in my youth group to negate my testimony for Christ or participate in any questionable activity. By personal conviction I will not attend motion picture theaters, including

drive-ins and cinerama; or any other program which
cannot be approved by a conscience which is daily
cleansed by the Word of God;

By personal conviction and as an elected officer and
leader in my youth group I will not attend dances as
a participant or as an observer, nor will I purchase
or listen to records which cannot be approved by a
conscience which is cleansed by the Word of God;
(Rock 'n Roll and Country in particular).

By personal conviction I will not use tobacco in any
form.

By personal conviction and as an elected leader in my
youth group, I will not use drugs in any form without
a prescription from a licensed doctor, nor will I use
marijuana;

By personal conviction and as an elected leader in my
youth group, I will not play cards;

By personal conviction I will not date the unsaved;

By personal conviction I will not abuse my privileges
as a driver of an automobile, if such a privilege is
mine;

By personal conviction my conduct on dates with a
Christian shall be discreet and above reproach. I
will date only Christians who are right and not
backslidden;

By personal conviction, as a boy, I will not wear my
hair too long at a questionable length (over eyebrows,
ears and collar), where I would be a stumblingblock;

By personal conviction, as a girl, I will wear my
dresses no higher than the top of the knee. I will
not wear slacks or shorts to school or any public
place;

By personal conviction I will not go mixed swimming
with the opposite sex (unless on a family outing),
nor will I go to a public swimming area;

I will flee youthful lusts and follow righteousness,
faith, charity, and peace with them that call on
the Lord of a pure heart;

I will not walk in the counsel of the ungodly,
nor stand in the way of sinners, nor sit in the
seat of the scornful but my delight shall be in
the law of the Lord;

I will back the Bible Club at my school 100 percent
by attendance and by urging others to do likewise.

I take the above covenant of office without any
mental reservation, and if I knowingly neglect my

spiritual life, I shall voluntarily request that
the Guard of Honor declare my office vacant and
that another be given my responsibilities.

Signed _____

Date _____

MONTHLY REPORT

(To be filled out by all leaders in the Trinity Baptist
Church Youth Program)

As a leader you are to score yourself 10 points for each question
in the affirmative. If your average for any one month falls below
70, the Guard of Honor may require you to appear before them and
give a reasonable account for your failure.

1. Have you had a consistent "Quiet Time" this past month?_____

2. Have you been faithful in attendance at the morning and evening
    worship services, Sunday school, Sunday evening Training Union
    Hour, and Prayer Meeting on Wednesday?_____

3. Where are you now reading in your Bible?_____

4. Have you led a soul to Christ this past month?_____

5. Have you witnessed to some lost soul this past month in a direct
    manner?_____

6. Have you been faithful in the visitation program?_____

7. Have you tithed your income to this church (this means parental
    allowance or earned money)?_____

8. Have you been faithful in discharging the duties of the office
    to which you have been elected?_____

9. Has your time spent in church activities been placed ahead in
    all other activities at school or at work (the only exception
    is the home)?_____

10. Have you been faithful to your Covenant of Office?_____

                        TOTAL_____

                        _____
                                  SIGNED

                        _____
                                   DATE

14 — Goals of a Successful Youth Ministry

In order to experience real success with teenagers, youth leaders must establish definite goals. These goals should be set at the beginning of every year and should involve every area of the ministry, including the following:

1. Goals for Sunday School:
   a. To have greater attendance.
   b. To challenge teachers to grow through their classes and to improve their teaching.
   c. To see teenagers advance in the Word of God.
   d. To develop or better a more interesting curriculum.
   e. To plan several "special days" in order to reach many new teenagers with the Gospel (include a special speaker and a reward for the teenager who brings the most visitors).

2. Goals for Soul Winning:
   a. Set a goal for every week.
   b. Set a goal for small and large groups.
   c. Set a goal even if souls are not saved every week. (In our first year at Trinity Baptist Church, the faithful teenagers numbered from 5 to 15. From these faithful few, the soul-winning outreach has grown to 80 to 100 who every week tell people about Jesus Christ. The first few months no one was saved, but suddenly souls began to be saved weekly; now a week never passes without a teenager leading someone to the Lord.)

3. Goals for Activities:
   a. Set goals one year in advance.
   b. Set goals to have a large turn-out of teenagers.
   c. Set goals to begin and end the activity on time.
   d. Set goals to establish unity within the group.
   e. Set goals to keep teenagers from worldly influences.
   f. Set goals to provide a good time for the young people (better than the world can give them in sin).
   g. Set goals to provide teens an opportunity to learn how to get along with others.
   h. Set goals to provide teens an opportunity to serve the Lord by—
      (1) Winning souls
      (2) Studying God's Word
      (3) Fellowshipping with Christians

4. Goals for Individual Lives:
   a. Set goals for your own life.
      (1) Have a good husband-wife relationship for teenagers to observe.
      (2) Have daily Bible reading and prayer.
      (3) Lead people to Christ weekly.
      (4) Lead new converts to make an open profession.
      (5) Be on time to all services.
      (6) Be dependable in every situation.
      (7) Train your children to have respect for others and to be well-behaved.
      (8) Do not neglect your children for your ministry but include them in your ministry.
      (9) Take time with your family.
      (10) Take time with the Lord.
   b. Set goals for teenagers.
      (1) See the lost teen saved.
      (2) See the teens involved in active service for the Lord.
      (3) See the teenagers become soul winners.
      (4) See them involved with the Word of God and prayer.

(5) See them unite with the church.
(6) See them have victory over sin and the world.
(7) See them live their teenage years without regretting the way they live.
(8) See them attend a Christian college after graduation.
(9) See them involved in full-time Christian service.

It is important that you youth ministers remember that you are not babysitters, but are endeavoring to build the lives of teenagers and to help them become usable in the hand of God; therefore, you must establish definite goals if the youth ministry is to be successful.

15 — The Youth Director's Wife: Help or Hindrance

By Nancy Reilly

"And the Lord God said, It is not good that the man should be alone; I will make him an help meet for him."—Gen. 2:18.

Since God created man and knows him better than man knows himself, we can take His Word for the authority that man needs a helpmeet to face the challenges of life.

Being the wife of any preacher of the Word is never easy, and I have no doubts that the life of the wife of a youth director is one of constant challenge and blessing! It is amazing how God can use a team of man and wife to serve Him more effectively.

Many years ago while we were first getting started in our ministry, I had to make a decision: should I remain the silent partner who tends to the home and waits patiently for a few moments at the end of each day to be with my husband; or should I join in with him, allowing his burden to become mine? I decided I wanted more than a few moments each day of my husband's life; I wanted to be a vital part of it. So began my part of the labors with teenagers. I cannot imagine not being involved in Ron's work! Of course, I have been blessed with a wonderful husband who wants me to be a part of his work. He has geared his ministry for this. We have truly been able to serve the Lord together.

I believe the biggest mistake any woman makes when working with her husband is in not making it clear to him and to others involved in the ministry that he is the boss; you are merely his helpmeet. Many times this is hard for folks to comprehend, especially if that has not been decided upon previously.

I remember one youth director who used to tell us, "I don't believe there is a place for my wife to be involved in my ministry. She belongs in the home, waiting for me!" He said this with great conviction, and we admired his strong determination to do it alone.

However, one year when he brought his wife and his young people with him to our winter retreat, I couldn't help noticing who was giving out the orders as to what ought to be done with the teenagers. Of course, you guessed it—the silent, housekeeping wife! No wonder that man thought his wife should be at home waiting for him; she just about took over his job when she was along! She was the ultimate loser because that was the one and only trip she ever made with her husband and the teenagers.

Taking an active part with one's youth-director husband also solves many problems before they ever can begin. The adolescent girl many times is intrigued with an older man and develops a "crush" on him. This is not an unusual experience at all and not necessarily a bad one, either. Many fathers of our teenage girls are not Christians, or else they do not live like Christians. Because of death or divorce, some girls do not even have a father in the home. These girls have never had a good, godly example of what a man can and should be like. They seem to need an outside influence to whom they can look, someone to observe and pattern their lives after. Their personal goals for a happy home need to be clearly seen and realized in the lives of the youth pastor and his wife.

The highest compliment a teenage girl can give to me is, "I want to have a husband who loves the Lord and me just like Brother Reilly loves the Lord and you!" It is always a thrill to hear a girl say this, and surely we have accomplished one of our biggest goals by giving them a godly and right image to follow.

There are times when a wife can discern even better than her husband one of the teenage girl's biggest problems. Oftentimes girls have female problems that would be embarrassing to talk over with their youth director, but not difficult at all to tell a woman.

If one has small children, it is especially difficult to leave them to go on all of the youth activities. There will always be critical women in the church who will say, "Your husband is working you too hard," or, "You should not be away from your children so much," or offer other "comforting" words. However, I decided that one day my sons will leave me for lives of their own (and wives of their own!). It is a foolish woman who makes no part for herself in her husband's ministry, and then is alone and struggling to find a place of service after her chickens have left the nest!

I am not advocating a woman's deserting her children or going out and working a job while she has children at home. On the contrary, I believe Mother ought to be in the home with her children; but on those weekly activities and teenage visitation, it is good for both child and mother to get out and be useful to others, especially her husband! Then when you have those few, precious moments together alone, you know exactly what your man has had to cope with, the burdens he bears, and the prayers he has for the different teenagers in your group.

Your children soon learn, too, how very important Daddy's work and ministry is and the responsibility that both Mom and Dad have with the young people. I don't remember a time when our boys, Ronnie and Jon Michael, haven't asked, "How many did the teenagers have saved tonight?"

When our ministry first began, it was quite expensive to pay a babysitter. Many times it was with great sacrifice, but we believed it important that I be there in the activities. The Lord moved on the heart of the pastor to have the church pay a babysitter and any other expenses that we would have while on an activity. This has been a great blessing.

If you intend to help your husband, there are liabilities involved in the job. You become an easier target when you "stick your neck out" and get involved. Many times people will be afraid to verbally attack your husband because he is a God-called preacher, but you are just his wife and an easy target. This keeps you on your toes, however, and teaches you that you do have the responsibility to be what the Bible teaches about a Christian woman.

Of course, you should have made it clear to everyone that you are not the leader—just the wife of the leader. You are merely carrying out his instructions and orders, not yours! This will make your job much easier.

Many times teenagers will ask, "Where are we going after such and such?" or, "What do we do when such and such happens?" I have replied hundreds of times, "I don't know; ask Brother Reilly!" thereby making it clear who the leader and boss is.

Once after giving my famous answer, a teenage boy said to me, "You don't know much, do you?" I assured him that I didn't, but Brother Reilly did and would be glad to help him!

I have been blessed with a husband who does protect me from the attacks of merciless people, but I would be negligent not to tell you that sometimes the darts get through even his protective shield of love, and they do hurt! But, oh, to know that you are sharing the pain with the one you love and the one God gave to you to help here on earth is the greatest medicine I can think of! Of course, the everlasting arms of our Lord Jesus are always there to give comfort and protection when the going gets tough!

Another responsibility I have had is to give a talk to our girls at our three teenage weeks of camp and our National Youth Conference. This talk is on the rules we have for a girl's dress while at the camp and why we have the rules. It is always exciting to take the Word of God and share the Bible principles of modesty with teenage girls and see the Holy Spirit verify what I have taught in their own hearts. I have had countless girls tell me that they had never had anyone tell them those things before, and that the Lord used me to challenge them to dress and conduct themselves as young, Christian ladies!

A big factor in assisting your husband as a youth leader is to learn to keep your mouth closed. Oftentimes it is tempting to share some inside news to a friend or parent to make a point about your ministry and the need for it in the lives of teenagers in the church. However, it isn't the wife's job to burden the hearts of the people to back the youth program. That's the job of the Holy Spirit.

I have seen many a youth pastor's wife get herself into an awkward position merely by telling too much. Often you will know things about a young person that very few people are aware of or have any knowledge of whatsoever. Therefore, it is imperative that you refrain from sharing your secrets with anyone but the Lord and your husband. When the youth worker's wife gets a reputation for telling too much, she jeopardizes her husband's ministry and is a hindrance to the cause of Christ.

I believe the wife of a youth leader (be he a full-time youth pastor or youth director or a layman who leads the teenagers) must be extra cautious of the way she dresses. I never cease to be amazed over the fact that the way a woman looks speaks more loudly than everything she teaches and her husband preaches.

Now just because a woman dresses modestly does not mean she cannot look attractive. On the contrary, I believe a modest Christian woman can be more attractive than the average woman on the street. Many Christian girls think that to be a good Christian lady one has to "give up" on looking good. The Devil fools many a girl into thinking only unsaved or ungodly women can be nice looking. I believe it is more glorifying to the Lord for a woman to dress modestly and attractively to show young girls that being a Christian does not mean we have to look pathetic and old and haggard. A good, modest, Christian lady and teenager can set the pace and have even the lost world respecting her in regard to her dress.

Then I have known some youth worker's wives who felt that they needed to dress like a teenager while in their forties! This is totally ridiculous; and the woman who does so is fooling no one, especially the teenager. There are some clothes that, even though modest, are inappropriate for a woman out of her teenage years.

It is also important for the youth director's wife to always hold her husband up as the example of what a Christian ought to be or do. Never criticize your husband to a teenager, and never disagree with him publicly. Remember, you are teaching the teenage girls how to respond to their husbands when they marry and also how to respect them. Save your opinions for when the two of you are completely alone and have time for discussions.

It is likewise important to hold up your husband to your own children. Always explain the importance of Daddy's work and how we must try to help him by the way we live. Don't constantly be burdening down your man with detail problems that he cannot do anything about at the time anyway. Try to work out the little time-consuming, detailed problems on your own and spare him a little needless pain.

The most important quality a woman needs in order to assist and to help her husband is a close, personal relationship with the Lord Jesus. Many a girl has tried to ride on the spirituality of her guy, only to be defeated and to pull her man down spiritually. Nothing takes the place of your own time alone in the Scriptures daily and your own daily prayer life with the Lord.

The thrilling thought is that as a youth director's wife you have a place of service in the Lord's work, a place where God can use you, a place where you can fulfill God's plan for your life.

"Who can find a virtuous woman? for her price is far above rubies. The heart of her husband doth safely trust in her, so that he shall have no need of spoil. She will do him good and not evil all the days of her life."—Prov. 31:10-12.

16 — The Youth Director and His Family

Helping others at the expense of one's own family is too great a price to pay. The Lord has never called upon a man to respond to the needs of others by neglecting the needs of his own family. In fact, the Bible clearly teaches that a man who does not provide for his own is worse than an infidel. I believe that this not only applies to monetary matters, but also involves the emotional and spiritual needs of each family member.

Preachers' children, or "PK's" as they are often called, are the spectators and see Dad and Mom make many sacrifices, and too little do they see the rewards involved. While an adult can wait for the rewards until he sees Christ and knows it will be worth it all, a child should not be expected to be spiritually or emotionally mature to endure to the end!

Your children constantly need to be made aware of the benefits and advantages of being a "PK." My sons now are advanced skiers only because they had the privilege of being a preacher's kid and of going on the ski trips we took with our teenagers. From the time that they were very small, Ron and Jon were taught to win souls. When Ronnie entered the youth group, he was far ahead of his peers in soul-winning experience because Dad took him soul winning with him on many occasions. This is not to say that we should spoil our children, but that we should take an active interest in their development as a person and as a Christian.

I have seen preachers' children who had no discipline whatever. It is very hard for a man's congregation or youth group to have confidence in the preacher if he does not have his own family in subjection with all authority.

Our children should not be expected to be perfect, but we should apply biblical principles and train them in the way they should go.

As a child approaches his teenage years, he needs to know that he can tell Dad anything. Keep the line of communication open. Some preachers' children are terrified of their father. They have been told so often not to do such and such because it would hurt Daddy's ministry that they are afraid to verbalize their fears and thoughts. Many times they become sneaks and do as they like. They decide that what Daddy doesn't know won't hurt him!

God judged Eli for not having his sons in subjection, and his ministry was brought to nought. God help us not to provoke our children to wrath.

The greatest reward a preacher can have is to have his children love and honor him.

The preacher and his family can exemplify the church and Christ's relationship. God grant it to be so in our homes and ministries.

17 — Parents

(The Key to Building the Teen's Life)

What a responsibility it is to be a parent! If a youth director is ever to accomplish anything of value in the life of a teenager, he *must* have the aid of parents. The life of the teen must be built in the home by the parents; the right kind of youth ministry must support those parents in order to be the means of providing the teenagers the best possible kind of life. This life can be a reality if several areas are developed in the home.

You parents must be rightly related to each other. Your children should be able to observe that Mom and Dad love each other because of the way you act and talk. Remember that saying which is so very true, *"Actions speak louder than words."* Your teenagers should hear you expressing your love for each other. One of the most detrimental forces to a teenager is the constant arguing and disagreeing of parents. This arguing will cause deep problems in a teenager's heart and might even cause him to hate the home and the church.

A second area which must be developed is the relationship between the parents and the teen. In order to be successful in this area, you must take the time necessary to really know your children. It is important to communicate with the child and to talk with him at every opportunity—not just when disciplining him! Allow the child to discuss freely and don't be shocked at what you hear. If there is more than one child in the family, take all of the children on outings together, and, on occasion, take each child on an outing by himself. These outings could consist of going hunting or fishing, if the child is a boy, and going shopping or walking in the park, if the child is a girl. This special attention will definitely help to keep open the lines of communication between you and your teenagers.

Parents, give your teenagers responsibilities to fulfill in the home. Give them specific jobs and expect them to do those jobs. Goals such as the following should be established for each teen, and you should encourage and aid him in accomplishing these goals:

1. To be a soul winner.
2. To read his Bible on a personal basis daily.
3. To do his best in school.
4. To be obedient to all authority.
5. To speak first to adults.
6. To keep his room clean.
7. To finish his job.
8. To tell the truth at all times.
9. To have spiritual and well-behaved friends.
10. To further his education in a Christian college.

Another important area to develop is your relationship with the Lord. Parents cannot expect children to be faithful or to walk with the Lord if your own lives do not demonstrate that you are walking with the Lord yourselves. Read the Bible and pray daily. Father, lead in daily devotions, but each individual member should also meet with God alone in his time of personal devotions. The key to all of this is that of being consistent so that the teenager will recognize that the Lord is real to each of you and that each of you means business for Him.

Another area to be considered is that which deals with your responsibility. Train your children in the Lord. Proverbs 22:6 states, "Train up a child in the way he should go: and when he is old, he will not depart from it." In Ephesians 6:4 the Bible states that there are two ways to bring up children—"nurture and admonition." The word "nurture" means to "support during the stages of growth." When a child becomes a teenager, it is not the time to think that he is completely grown and therefore needs no more parental guidance. Rather, he is still growing physically, emotionally, and spiritually; and during this stage, he needs more guidance, advice and support from you than ever before.

Prayerfully guide your teenager by the Word of God; advise him or her as one who is interested in the youth's spiritual well-being, and support the young person by encouraging him or her to be involved in the youth activities of the church.

PARENTS OF TODAY

Oh, parents, have you stopped to think
  You hold a sacred place?
That child of yours: will he thank God
  You told him of God's grace?

Or will the future have to be,
  "Where is my child today?"
Because you had no thought of God,
  You lived for self your way.

You did not do things very bad,
  You had no time to pray.
You do have time for worldly things,
  But none for God today.

You lead your child the way you go,
  For self at any cost;
Then find out when it is too late
  Your child and you are lost.

How comforting it is to know
  You taught your child to pray,
To read the blessed Word of God
  And live for God each day.

By word and life to love God's house
  For worship, prayer and praise,
Until you meet with all the saved
  For everlasting days.

Author Unknown

The word "admonition" means "to notify or reprove for a fault." If you are to bring your children up right, you must give admonition to teens when it is needed. This can be accomplished by love and discipline. Proverbs 29:15,17 tells us, "The rod and reproof give wisdom: but a child left to himself bringeth his mother to shame. Correct thy son, and he shall give thee rest; yea, he shall give delight unto thy soul."

Today young people seem to have the idea that no one can tell them what to do. They feel that they should not be punished for anything which they have done wrong. I like the old-fashioned method as expressed in this poem:

> Junior bit the meter man.
> Junior kicked the cook,
> Junior's anti-social now
>   (According to the book).
>
> Junior smashed the clock and lamp.
> Junior hacked the tree.
> (Destructive trends are treated
>   In chapters two and three).
>
> Junior threw his milk at Mom.
> Junior screamed for more.
> (Notes of self-assertiveness
>   Are found in chapter four).
>
> Junior tossed his shoes and socks
>   Out into the rain.
> (Negation, that, and normal—
>   Disregard the stain).
>
> Junior got in Grandpop's room,
>   Tore up his fishing line.
> That's to gain attention. . .
>   (See page eighty-nine).
>
> Grandpop seized a slipper and
>   Yanked Junior 'cross his knee,
> (Grandpop hasn't read a book
>   Since 1893).
>
> Author Unknown

Good strong discipline in the home should be coupled with the instruction of a loving father and the tender care of a loving mother. When instruction is given, it will provide **wisdom** for the teenager. Proverbs 13:1 says, "A wise son heareth his father's instruction: but a scorner heareth not rebuke." In Proverbs 4:1, 5 to 13 we read,

"Hear, ye children, the instruction of a father, and attend to know understanding. . .

Get wisdom, get understanding: forget it not; neither decline from the words of my mouth.

Forsake her not, and she shall preserve thee: love her, and she shall keep thee. . . .

Exalt her, and she shall promote thee: she shall bring thee to honour, when thou dost embrace her .

She shall give to thine head an ornament of grace: a crown of glory shall she deliver to thee.

Hear, O my son, and receive my sayings; and the years of thy life shall be many.

I have taught thee in the way of wisdom; I have led thee in right paths.

When thou goest, thy steps shall not be straitened; and when thou runnest, thou shalt not stumble.

Take fast hold of instruction; let her not go: keep her; for she is thy life."

Instruction will **protect** the teenager—Proverbs 2:10-19:

"When wisdom entereth into thine heart, and knowledge is pleasant unto thy soul;

Discretion shall preserve thee, understanding shall keep thee:

To deliver thee from the way of the evil man, from the man that speaketh froward things;

Who leave the paths of uprightness, to walk in the ways of darkness;

Who rejoice to do evil, and delight in the frowardness of the wicked;

Whose ways are crooked, and they froward in their paths:

To deliver thee from the strange woman, even from the stranger which flattereth with her words;

Which forsaketh the guide of her youth, and forgetteth the covenant of her God.

For her house inclineth unto death, and her paths unto the dead.

None that go unto her return again, neither take they hold of the paths of life."

Instruction will **instill** character and prove a father's love. "Open rebuke is better than secret love" (Prov. 27:5). And Proverbs 29:15,17 says, "The rod and reproof give wisdom: but a child left to himself bringeth his mother to shame. Correct thy son, and he shall give thee rest; yea, he shall give delight unto thy soul."

You parents also have a responsibility to obey the spiritual leadership of the church which you attend. Hebrews 13:17 tells us, "Obey them that have the rule over you, and submit yourselves: for they watch for your souls, as they that must give account, that they may do it with joy, and not with grief: for that is unprofitable for you."

The pastor and youth director should be upheld by prayer and should be supported by you parents before your teens. Many teenagers have been lost to the world because parents continually criticized the youth director and made it impossible for the teen to trust or respect his authority over him. You who want the best for your teenager will make certain that the teen is totally involved in the youth program and will support the program and its leaders.

When Christian parents rear their children in the Bible way, there are rewards which they will reap, not only at the judgment seat of Christ, but also here in this life. The home will have peace and harmony. Psalm 128:3 promises, "Thy wife shall be as a fruitful vine by the sides of thine house: thy children like olive plants round about thy table." The children will be a blessing instead of a curse. Psalm 127:3-5 tells us,

"Lo, children are an heritage of the Lord: and the fruit of the womb is his reward. As arrows are in the hand of a mighty man; so are children of the youth. Happy is the man that hath his quiver full of them: they shall not be ashamed, but they shall speak with the enemies in the gate."

You parents will have joy in seeing your young people continue on for the Lord either as a full-time Christian worker or as a Christian layman who serves in a good church.

18 — Counseling Teenagers

If the youth director is doing his job correctly, he will have young people lined up wanting to talk with him. When he loves his teenagers and has a real burden for them, they will seek his advice and counsel.

Teenagers have basic needs common to all young people. And many times they seek counsel from the youth leader in the following areas:

1. The conflict with other people and the problem of how to get along.
2. The parental conflict is prevalent during many of the teen's years. Counselor, support the authority of the home while at the same time maintaining the teen's confidence. This wisdom comes from the Word of God. Ephesians 6:1,2 teaches, "Children, obey your parents in the Lord: for this is right. Honour thy father and mother; which is the first commandment with promise."
3. The lack of confidence is a very basic problem with *many* teens. Youth leader, convince them that their involvement with soul winning and with the youth activities will give them their needed confidence.
4. Disappointment of one's self image causes many to be unhappy with themselves. Make them realize those good characteristics and traits which God has given to them.
5. Unhappiness in the home disturbs many. As counselor, you should point out what the teen could do to improve his home.

6. Trouble in school is of concern to some.
7. Making of minor decisions causes some frustration.
8. Problems between boy and girl friends are very common and are a curse to youth groups. It is difficult to build unity within a group when boys and girls are building weak physical relationships with each other.
9. Personality conflicts are a source of trouble to some.
10. Discouragement which many experience may lead to depression.
11. Problems which listening to rock music causes are the most serious that teenagers will face. Teens will be tempted to listen to rock music, so they must be counselled with from God's Word if they are to have victory over this temptation. It is imperative that rock music be replaced with that which is of "good report."
12. The making of wrong friendships causes many to fail spiritually. In order to succeed and grow in the Lord, help them get rid of their bad friends and replace them with spiritual friends.

In addition to those common to most teenagers, many young people are involved in more serious problems.

1. "Fooling around" with drugs.
2. Taking drugs "all the way." If teens seek for help at this point, you counselors may need to seek outside help if the teens agree.
3. "Fooling around" with sex.
4. "All the way" into fornication.
5. Involved in perversion.
6. Feeling guilty from past sins of involvement in adultery, drugs, or some other fleshly sins.
7. Feeling of despondency.
8. Feeling of depression.
9. Running away from home.
10. Thinking of committing suicide. Some could have already attempted suicide or be involved in the act of doing so when they contact you. They might be desiring attention, but the counselor must not consider their

threats lightly. Much wisdom from the Lord and much knowledge from the Word of God is needed to counteract serious problems.

Teenagers within the youth group will have many spiritual problems for which they will seek counsel.

1. Bible questions.
2. Lack of assurance of salvation.
3. Disagreements with standards which the youth leader has established for the youth group.
4. God's will for their lives.
5. Problems with the world.
6. Problems with reading the Bible.
7. Problems with soul winning.
8. Future goals.
9. Fears of not succeeding.

Youth directors, give young people help from the Word of God and be careful not to put them off but give them the counseling they need. And it is necessary that you know how to counsel.

There are basically three stages in counseling.

The beginning stage consists of one or more interviews. The goal of this stage is to establish a good working relationship and a mutual trust. Become friends. Notice, I did not state that you are to become the teen's "big buddy." If a counselor becomes the teen's buddy, he must place himself on the teen's level in order to reach him; and when this occurs, the teen loses all respect for the counselor's authority. Exhibit a genuine love and concern for the teenager. In counseling teenage girls, be careful never to show your concern for them by giving them a big hug. Always follow a "no touch" rule in all of your dealings with teenage girls. The girls in my youth group never questioned my concern for them, and I never demonstrated my concern by any kind of physical contact. When the teen respects the director's position and senses his honest concern, he will then have confidence and trust in his counsel.

The second stage comes when the teen begins to share his

problems with you. The key, at this point, is "insight," and now you are able to work toward the cure.

The final stage involves the teen's independence and self direction. The counseling session is successful when the teen no longer is dependent upon you but takes full responsibility for his life and accepts himself as he is. He should be able to turn to and depend upon the Lord to meet his needs.

Follow a process in counseling in order to avoid wasting time or being too disorganized.

1. Prepare yourself. Be right with the Lord, and know the Word of God and how to use it.
2. Be a good listener. Allow the teen to talk; and as he talks, you should be able to gain knowledge as to the real problem. Listen for themes and then distinguish between the causes and symptoms in order to get to the real problem.
3. Don't appear shocked at anything you hear. Always believe what the teen tells you even if you doubt its validity.
4. Never argue with the teen.
5. Be careful not to degrade the teen for what he has revealed.
6. Do not overestimate the problem.
7. Help the teenager before he leaves. By reflecting upon the statements that have been made during the session, by tracing the problem to its source, and by dealing with the problem, you should be able to challenge him to solve his problem. Avoid making a hasty conclusion. Before the teen leaves the office, pray with him and let him know that he may return at any time for additional help.

The key to the relationship between counselor and teen is that everything he tells you remains strictly confidential.

Counselors may carry burdens which are difficult to bear; but in order to keep the teen's trust, you must not reveal what he has told in confidence. The youth leader will be loved and greatly respected by the teens with whom he works, even if they do not support his stand for the Bible and his adherence to biblical separation.

19 — Gideon's Band

(The Ultimate in Soul Winning)

"Then Jerubbaal, who is Gideon, and all the people that were with him, rose up early, and pitched beside the well of Harod: so that the host of the Midianites were on the north side of them, by the hill of Moreh, in the valley. And the Lord said unto Gideon, The people that are with thee are too many for me to give the Midianites into their hands, lest Israel vaunt themselves against me, saying, Mine own hand hath saved me."—Judges 7:1,2.

When the Lord gave us the burden to reach the masses on the beaches of Daytona over the Easter holidays, God wanted to get all the glory for the salvation of the lost. Humanly speaking, the way to reach more people with the Gospel is to have more people witnessing. But God chooses His own way of reaching people; and He has chosen teenagers, few in number but willing to be used, to win as many as 5,432 people to a saving knowledge of Jesus Christ in a three-day witnessing venture over the Easter holidays.

Years ago when our burden first became reality, I knew that not just any Christian teenager could be an effective witness on the beach. Over the Easter holidays Daytona Beach is the most difficult place in America to witness for Christ.

"And the Midianites and the Amalekites and all the children of the east lay along in the valley like grasshoppers for multitude; and their camels were without number, as the sand by the seaside for multitude."—Judges 7:12.

That portion of Scripture is as complete a picture of Daytona Beach over Easter as anyone could ever give. As far as the eye can see, multitudes are lying alongside the beach like grasshoppers, and their vans and cars and motorcycles are without number. People are there from every state and from all walks of life. The majority are high-school and college-age young people, but there are some families and older people, too—truly sand by the seaside for multitude. Police estimate the crowd at 500,000 over the Easter weekend. They are there from every race and religion, and these people are going to live somewhere forever. They need a Saviour. They live in America, yet they have never heard the story of God's amazing love in sending Christ Jesus into the world to save sinners.

I set up qualifications that the teenagers at Trinity Baptist Church must fulfill in order to go on the witnessing trip to Daytona. They:

1. Must be in the ninth grade or over.
2. Must come to all the services of the church.
3. Must come to all teen visitation and all youth activities.
4. Must memorize and be tested over a portion of Scripture.
5. Must have won at least ten souls to Christ within a set period.
6. Must bring three visitors to a service of the church.
7. Must attend the preparatory meetings on soul winning.
8. Girls must wear modest dress.
9. Boys must have proper, manly haircuts and wear slacks, shirt, shoes and socks.

Some have criticized the Bible requirements, but their argument is with God, for He clearly teaches in His Word that every one 'should know how to possess his vessel in sanctification and honour' (I Thess. 4:4). These qualifications are merely guidelines for the teenager who is desirous to do God's will and be a vessel fit for the Master's use.

It would take pages to tell the experiences that the young people have had while witnessing at Daytona. One thirty-one-year-old mother who received Christ as Saviour wept as she told how she was entering the hospital the following week for cancer surgery. The doctor had given little hope of her survival, and she was so concerned about her eternal destiny. She had been raised a Mormon, but never felt at peace with God and was ready for the Word to be sown in her heart. She took her three children—ages 10,12,14—from the ocean so that they could also hear how they might go to Heaven when they died. They, too, received Christ as their Saviour.

One of our teenage boys one year walked a seventy-year-old Catholic lady down the beach to her home and gave her the simple plan of salvation. At her door, she bowed her head and received forgiveness of sin and was gloriously saved.

Another college boy, age twenty, had been told by his doctors that he had six months to live and that his body was full of cancer. He trusted Christ and was saved.

One year the last person to get saved on the Daytona trip was a girl named Sherri who was twenty. She bowed her head while standing in the line at the cafeteria and asked Christ to forgive her sin and come into her heart. She ate with us and was given follow-up material and assurance of her salvation from God's Word.

God's Word takes effect in the hearts of people in a crowded restaurant, a sandy beach, or a street corner.

"And they stood every man in his place round about the camp: and all the host ran, and cried, and fled" (Judges 7:21). The teens stood every one in his place throughout Daytona, and the lost heard God's message of salvation and of His power to save from sin; many thousands received the gift of eternal life and were born again. The young people from Trinity who have gone on these trips have proved that God is willing to save to the uttermost all who will come to Him. The burden of my heart is the untapped potential in America that God could use to reach the multitudes with the Gospel.

The results of the past thirteen years of witnessing at Daytona are as follows:

1st year...............233 saved
2nd year..............316 saved

3rd year ....481 saved
4th year ....541 saved
5th year ....852 saved
6th year ....1516 saved
7th year ....1615 saved
8th year ....2050 saved
9th year ....2643 saved
10th year ....3165 saved
11th year ....4044 saved
12th year ....5152 saved
13th year ....5432 saved
28,040 Total

The Word of God is quick and powerful, and it did its work on the beaches of Daytona. The young people were equipped with the finest equipment to be found—the Bible! As they approached people, they introduced themselves, then asked, "If you were to die today, do you know you would go to Heaven?" The power of God swept down and the convicting power of the Holy Spirit did His work in thousands of lives. Only eternity will reveal the other thousands who received a gospel witness and later trusted Christ. The names and addresses of those who are saved are recorded, and follow-up material is sent to each. A letter is enclosed, congratulating the new Christian on his accepting Christ and going over step by step how to be saved and how to have assurance. Included also are instructions telling the new Christian how to make a public profession in a Bible-preaching church. Each packet contains a Gospel of John.

The thrill to my heart is that teenagers are privileged to be used by God to win so many to Christ. I am filled with great anticipation as we expand this ministry to a national level and include teenagers from Bible-preaching churches in this outreach.

Teenagers from other churches must meet the same qualifications, and I will be working closely with pastors and youth directors, helping them to oversee their young people work for the opportunity of this witnessing venture. I thrill as I see spiritual growth of these teenagers who go on the trip. There is something about soul winning that warms the heart of a teen like nothing else. Ours know that they can be used by God to win souls while yet a teenager. The Devil cannot convince them that doing right and serving God is just for adults. Daytona is proof of that.

Praise the Lord for what He accomplishes in the lives of all who are saved and also in the lives and hearts of the many who make the trip to the beaches of Daytona. To God be the glory for the great victory He has given to us at Daytona Beach!

20 — Relationship Between
Pastor and Youth Director

In order for a youth ministry to be successful in accomplishing definite goals for teenagers, it is imperative that the line of communication between pastor and youth director be open and in good condition.

The youth director or youth pastor is not the pastor of the church; neither is the pastor of the church the youth director. Each of the two positions is a separate and distinct calling and ministry.

While I was preaching in a youth camp, God was blessing, and during the invitation many teenagers responded to the moving of the Holy Spirit.

After the service, a young youth director approached me and asked, "Why in the world are you just a youth director when you can preach like that!" I informed him that I was not just a youth director but a God-called preacher to teenagers!

A youth director has a sacred and holy responsibility to his calling. A youth leader doing his job could not possibly have time to be pastor of a church, for his job is totally consuming and fulfilling. As the youth group increases in number, it is necessary for the church to employ a full-time man to work with teenagers.

No woman should be a youth director. The Bible clearly teaches that women are not to be preachers (I Tim. 2:12). A woman can work with young people if she works under the direction of the youth director or youth pastor, but never should a woman be the leader of the youth ministry.

From the pulpit the pastor should teach and preach the necessity and importance of teenagers getting involved totally in the youth program. He should stress attendance to all youth activities and to youth visitation. If the pastor does not mention the youth ministry, he conveys the attitude that it really does not matter, and people will soon develop an attitude of indifference toward the youth program. The pastor in the pulpit is responsible for the place the youth ministry will hold in the church. As it has been said many times—everything rises and falls on leadership.

It is most important that the pastor and youth director have the same philosophy regarding the local church and youth ministry. A soul-winning youth program will not succeed in a church that is not a soul-winning church. And it is a tragedy in a soul-winning church to have the youth ministry based solely on "fun times" or "Bible studies." The youth ministry and adult program should complement each other.

One of the most detrimental factors to both the total church program and the youth ministry is if the teenagers surpass the adults in their efforts to reach the lost. Because of youth, a teenager may possess more stamina than an adult in a concentrated soul-winning effort, but never should the teenagers excel the adults in zeal and fervency to reach the lost. This is why it is so important that pastor and youth director work hand in hand even in their preaching efforts to challenge the total church family to be soul winners!

The youth ministry also needs the support of the pastor when he is both in and out of the pulpit. Often parents will not understand the position taken on a certain issue by the youth pastor, so they may request private meetings with the pastor and youth director. When these confrontations take place, pastor, always stand with your youth leader, and together present a united front. Unfortunately, I know of many youth leaders who, because of their stand on certain issues, came into conflict with parents or other leaders in the church. In too many cases the pastor did not support the youth director because he feared the displeasure of people.

It was not an accident that I remained at Trinity Baptist Church as a youth director for over thirteen years. My ministry could never have had God's blessing and success without the faithful support and backing of our pastor, Dr. Bob Gray. He has allowed me the freedom to develop my ministry. And he always made it clear to the people that we were in total agreement on our philosophy of working with parents.

To have a successful youth ministry, it is imperative that both pastor and youth director communicate and render the support and aid necessary to reach the lost teenagers of our land.